TEENS
Religion & Values

GAIL SNYDER

THE GALLUP YOUTH SURVEY:
MAJOR ISSUES AND TRENDS

Teens and Alcohol

Teens and Family Issues

Teens and Race

Teens, Religion, and Values

Teens and Sex

Teens and Suicide

TEENS
Religion & Values

GAIL SNYDER

Produced by OTTN Publishing, Stockton, New Jersey

Mason Crest Publishers
370 Reed Road
Broomall, PA 19008
www.masoncrest.com

First printing

1 3 5 7 9 8 6 4 2

Library of Congress Cataloging-in-Publication Data

Snyder, Gail.
    Teens, religion, and values / Gail Snyder.
      p. cm. — (The Gallup Youth Survey, major issues and trends)
      Summary: Uses data from the Gallup Youth Survey and other sources to
   examine the issue of teen values and religious beliefs in today's world.
      Includes bibliographical references and index.
      ISBN 1-59084-726-1
   1. Teenagers—Religious life—United States—Juvenile literature.
   [1. Teenagers—Religious life. 2. Conduct of life.] I. Title. II. Series.
     BL625.47.S69 2004
     200'.835'0973—dc22

                                        2003018379

Contents

Introduction

By George Gallup

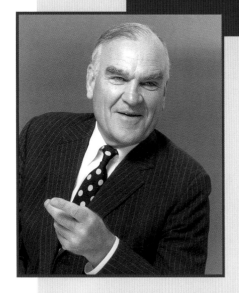

As the United States moves into the new century, there is a vital need for insight into what it means to be a young person in America. Today's teenagers—the so-called "Y Generation"—will be the leaders and shapers of the 21st century. The future direction of the United States is being determined now in their hearts and minds and actions. Yet how much do we as a society know about this important segment of the U.S. populace who have the potential to lift our nation to new levels of achievement and social health?

The nation's teen population will top 30 million by the year 2006, the highest number since 1975. Most of these teens will grow up to be responsible citizens and leaders. But some youths face very long odds against reaching adulthood physically safe, behaviorally sound, and economically self-supporting. The challenges presented to society by the less fortunate youth are enormous. To help meet these challenges it is essential to have an accurate picture of the present status of teenagers.

The Gallup Youth Survey—the oldest continuing survey of teenagers—exists to help society meet its responsibility to youth, as well as to inform and guide our leaders by probing the social and economic attitudes and behaviors of young people. With theories abounding about the views, lifestyles, and values of adolescents, the Gallup Youth Survey, through regular scientific measurements of teen themselves, serves as a sort of reality check.

We need to hear more clearly the voices of young people, and to help them better articulate their fears and their hopes. Our youth have much to share with their elders—is the older generation really listening? Is it carefully monitoring the hopes and fears of teenagers today? Failure to do so could result in severe social consequences.

Surveys reveal that the image of teens in the United States today is a negative one. Teens are frequently maligned, misunderstood, or simply ignored by their elders. Yet two decades of the Gallup Youth Survey have provided ample evidence of the very special qualities of the nation's youngsters. In fact, if our society is less racist, less sexist, less polluted, and more peace loving, we can in considerable measure thank our young people, who have been on the leading edge on these issues.

And the younger generation is not geared to greed: survey after survey has shown that teens have a keen interest in helping those people, especially in their own communities, who are less fortunate than themselves

Young people tell the Gallup Youth Survey that they are enthusiastic about helping others, and are willing to work for world peace and a healthy world. They feel positive about their schools and even more positive about their teachers. A large majority of American teenagers report that they are happy and excited about the future, feel very close to their families, are likely to marry, want to have children, are satisfied with their personal lives, and desire to reach the top of their chosen careers.

But young adults face many threats, so parents, guardians, and concerned adults must commit themselves to do everything possible to help tomorrow's parents, citizens, and leaders avoid or overcome risky behaviors so that they can move into the future with greater hope and understanding.

The Gallup Organization and the Gallup Youth Survey are enthusiastic about this partnership with Mason Crest Publishers. Through carefully and clearly written books on a variety of vital topics dealing with teens, Gallup Youth Survey statistics are presented in a way that gives new depth and meaning to the data. The focus of these books is a practical one—to provide readers with the statistics and solid information that they need to understand and to deal with each important topic.

* * *

Any examination of the lives of U.S. teenagers would be incomplete without careful consideration of the spirituality and religiosity of this age group. Indeed, probably the best way to safeguard teens today from the risks they face is to arm them with a strong faith and a solid set of values.

This is a surprising generation, with teens more traditional than their elders in a number of ways. Teens want to reduce the violence on television; they feel divorce should be harder to get; they want tougher laws against drinking and driving. Interestingly, these traditional views of teens are coupled with expansive views about their future role in the world. Most young people see their generation contributing to a world that is more tolerant, less polluted, more peaceful, and more concerned about the needs of people who are less fortunate than they.

This book offers guidance to teenagers on ways to integrate faith with their concerns about sex, marriage, and parenting. It explores how teens strive for guidelines in a society that seems to encourage unethical behavior and spawn negative role models.

Chapter One

Columbine High School students stand before memorial crosses for the 12 teenagers and 1 teacher murdered by students Eric Harris and Dylan Klebold in April 1999. The Christian victims of the attacks were martyrs in the eyes of many young people.

Columbine's Martyrs

Misty and Brad Bernall knew they needed to move their daughter, Cassie, away from the neighborhood. They had already placed her in a Christian private school in Lakewood, Colorado, hoping to separate her from a set of friends regarded as bad influences. In the fall of Cassie's freshman year in 1996, she had been cutting classes and earning Ds and Fs. She had also been using drugs and making threats to run away and kill herself.

Even more troubling, Misty had recently discovered some letters to Cassie in her bedroom. The letters from Cassie's best friend contained plans to murder a teacher and graphic illustrations of disemboweled people. One of the letters said, "Kill your parents! Murder is the answer to all of your problems. Make those scumbags pay for our suffering."

When the concerned Bernalls contacted the authorities and the parents of Cassie's friends,

Cassie was furious. What followed was a period in which Cassie hated her parents and rebelled against the tight restrictions on whom she could see. In an essay for English class, Cassie wrote, "Throughout this time I hated my parents and God with the deepest, darkest hatred. There are no words that can accurately describe the blackness I felt. . . ."

But then, at her new private school, Cassie met a new friend who invited her to attend a youth retreat in the nearby Rocky Mountains with 300 other teens. The Bernalls reluctantly decided to let Cassie go on the trip. When she returned, they could not believe the change in her. Her father remembered:

> When she left she had still been this gloomy, head-down, say-nothing girl. But that day—the day she came back—she was bouncy and excited about what happened to her. It was as if she had been in a dark room, and somebody had turned the light on, and she could suddenly see the beauty surrounding her.

For Cassie, the weekend was a rebirth. She gradually began participating in more youth group activities such as ski trips and weekly Bible study classes with her newfound religious friends. But despite her recent turnaround, Cassie was not happy attending the Christian school and asked her parents if she could transfer to Columbine High School in Littleton. Pleased with the changes she had made and satisfied with Columbine's reputation, the Bernalls agreed to let Cassie transfer.

Rachel Scott was another Columbine student who had a religious awakening before coming to the high school. When Rachel was 12 years old, relatives took her to a Pentecostal church during her stay in Shreveport, Louisiana. She later wrote in her journal about the unforgettable experience: "That night, I accepted Jesus into my heart. I was saved." As she grew older, Rachel became active as a leader in a Christian youth ministry group called

Breakthrough. She often made sacrifices, sometimes leaving early from her after-school job at a Subway restaurant to attend the group's meetings on Monday and Wednesday evenings. She had dreams of being a missionary and was looking forward to participating in a mission trip to Africa in the summer of 1999.

While Cassie and Rachel were finding strength from their

On April 20, 1999, Eric Harris (left) and Dylan Klebold took their own lives after murdering fellow students and a teacher at Columbine High School in Littleton, Colorado.

faiths, two Columbine students were struggling with their inner demons. Unlike many of their peers, Eric Harris and Dylan Klebold ultimately failed to deal with the pressures they experienced as adolescents. On April 20, 1999, the paths of Harris and Klebold crossed with those of Cassie, Rachel, and other high school students in Littleton, in what was one of the most tragic days in American history.

Harris, 18, and Klebold, 17, were part of a group called the Trenchcoat Mafia, which earned its name because its members wore long black trench coats. The students in the small faction were alienated from their classmates and had been the subject of taunts and derision for some time. In home videos Harris and Klebold recorded in the spring of 1999, they lashed out at the school's Christian students, as well as minorities and popular athletes. And on that April day, Christian teenagers were among the 12 students whom the pair shot and killed.

Thirteen Tears Watering a Rose

For the students and teachers at Columbine High School in Littleton, Colorado, April 20, 1999, started as a typical day. Outside the school, the long Colorado winter had finally broken and students were able to wear shorts to school for the first time. Inside the school, the chorus prepared for a concert later that day. A biology class took a test. Harris and Klebold had made a secret suicide pact and chose this day to carry out their plans. Before the day was over, they intended to take their own lives. Before doing that, the two boys planned to kill their classmates as well.

The attacks began at 11:30 A.M. when Harris and Klebold calmly walked onto the school grounds armed with four guns and some 30 homemade bombs, then began methodically shooting their way through hallways and classrooms. Police arrived on the scene within minutes, but were unable to enter the school because Klebold and Harris had booby-trapped some of the doors. They had even wired explosive devices to themselves. The carnage ended some three hours later in the school library. Along with the 13 people whom the boys killed — one of them a teacher — 28 more students were injured in the attack. Harris and Klebold made sure to save two bullets, and at the end of a long shooting spree, they turned their guns on themselves.

Klebold and Harris found Cassie Bernall in the high school library, where she had been struggling over Shakespeare's *Macbeth* before the shooting began. Many teens had hid under desks after hearing the gunshots and hoped the killers would ignore them. One young man, a sophomore, was watching from under a desk, not far from where Cassie was hiding. He later recalled hearing the exchange between Cassie and the attackers:

> I couldn't see anything when those guys came up to Cassie, but I could recognize her voice. I could hear everything like it was right next to me. One of them asked her if she believed in God. She paused, like she didn't know what she was going to answer, and then she said yes. She must have been scared, but her voice didn't sound shaky. It was strong. Then they asked her why, though they didn't give her a chance to respond. They just blew her away.

Elsewhere, many of the terrified students found the courage to perform incredible acts of heroism. A young man who had been shot multiple times lobbed one of the bombs away from other students before it detonated. Many students did everything they could to help Dave Sanders, the science teacher who was mortally wounded. Boys gave him the shirts off their backs to serve as pillows and bandages. They prayed for him, refusing

Rachel Scott, remembered on this cross raised in Littleton after the Columbine attacks, was an outspoken Christian. Witnesses reported that she declared her faith immediately before her classmates shot her.

to leave his side before the paramedics finally arrived hours after he had been shot.

Lexis Coffey-Berg, a Columbine student, remembered many teens praying during the attack. "In a world where there are so many religions," she said, "everyone was praying the same way." There was quiet prayer being held in the school's choir room, where students were mindful that any noise could attract the attention of the killers. Recalled Craig Nason, a junior, "I was terrified on the outside. But on the inside, God gave me peace. I felt like many others outside the school were praying for us." In the library, where most of the carnage took place, Seth Houy used his body to cover his sister and her friend. They were not hit by any bullets. "Honestly, I think that God made us invisible," he told a reporter. "We prayed the hardest we'd ever prayed, and God put an invisible shield around us."

Craig Scott, Rachel Scott's brother, was also in the library hiding between Isaiah Shoels and Matt Kechter. Craig watched in horror as both students were shot to death. When he fled the library, he took other students with him. Once they were safe, they began praying for their brothers and sisters who were in the school that day. When some of the teens were reunited with their siblings, Craig said, "'See, I told you, I told you prayer worked. I told you your sister was going to come out of this,' I said—and they thanked me."

Craig feared, though, that his sister Rachel had not been so lucky. The killers found Rachel Scott eating lunch outside in the sunshine. Witnesses said that, as with Cassie, Rachel's last words affirmed her faith in God. She kept a diary in which she wrote letters to God. The last entry in the journal was made just 20 minutes before her death. One of the bullets that killed her passed through her backpack and left a hole in her journal.

Rachel's journal writings show her gratitude to God and her impending sense that her life would soon be cut short. Eleven months before she died she wrote in her journal: "This will be my last year Lord. I have gotten what I can. Thank you." Although they knew that her love of God was strong, her parents were still surprised at what they found when they read her final journal

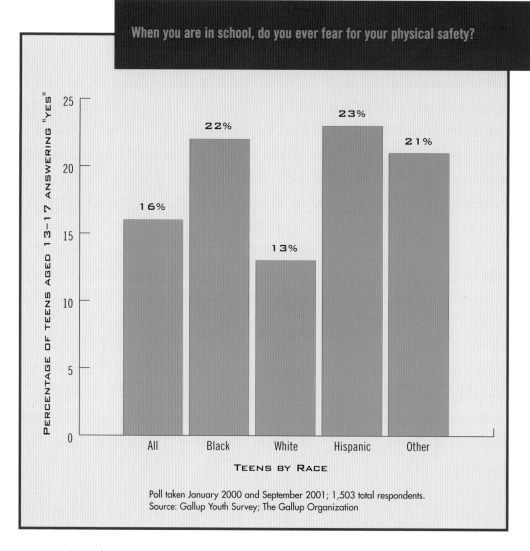

Poll taken January 2000 and September 2001; 1,503 total respondents.
Source: Gallup Youth Survey; The Gallup Organization

entry. Inside was a key to a mystery that had developed shortly after her death.

Her father, Darryl Scott, had reported getting a call after Rachel's funeral from a stranger from Ohio named Frank Amedia. He told Scott that he had wanted to share a dream that he had recently had about Rachel. In the dream, Amedia saw teardrops flowing from Rachel's eyes, and he believed the tears were about to give life to something. Amedia expected Scott would know what the dream meant, though he did not.

When the police returned Rachel's diary, her father reported being dumbstruck. On the last page was a drawing of Rachel's eyes and her 13 tears watering a rose. Afterwards, when Scott revisited her other diaries he discovered a similar picture, drawn the year before. In the picture a rose grew out of a columbine plant, a kind of buttercup flower, and it also had an inscription that read: "Greater love hath no man than this, that a man would

Melted seats in Columbine's cafeteria reveal some of the damage of the bombs that Eric Harris and Dylan Klebold set off.

lay down his life for his friends." Scott said, "I was so stunned that I could barely breathe. A week ago, a complete stranger who lived more than one thousand miles away had described exactly what I was looking at in Rachel's final diary!"

On one of the videotapes Harris and Klebold made prior to the shooting, they speculated that director Steven Spielberg might one day make a movie about them. That hasn't happened. Instead of achieving notoriety for themselves, Harris and Klebold and their cold-blooded actions set in motion a far different outcome than they could have imagined: they created several teenage Christian martyrs whose steadfast belief in God in the face of such violence inspired a religious resurgence on high school campuses across the nation.

Cassie Bernall, Rachel Scott, and the students praying during the attacks were not unlike many young people who have discovered the power and values of faith. Many studies show that today an overwhelming majority of teenagers believe in God and that they worship regularly. The Gallup Organization, an international polling firm, has long been interested in the religious practices of young people. Over the years, the organization has posed many questions to teenagers about religion and values through the Gallup Youth Survey, a long-term study that gauges young people's attitudes and beliefs.

Word of Cassie Bernall's testimony quickly spread after her death. A Gallup Youth Survey conducted in the fall of 1999 found that 69 percent of teens knew that Cassie died at Columbine because she said she believed in God. More than half the teens surveyed found personal meaning in the tragedy. They agreed that Cassie's example strengthened their own faith in God. *Time* magazine reported that in dozens of states, hundreds of evangelical teens gathered in her name.

Many teens felt like Susan Teran, a sixth-grader at Marshall Middle School in Wichita, Kansas. She said, "If there was a shooter at my school, I'd volunteer to sacrifice my life. I'd say, 'Don't shoot my friends; shoot me,' because I know where I'll go when I die."

Chapter Two

Catholic teens unite for a rally during World Youth Day, a massively attended annual celebration. Research shows that today's teens are as devoted to their religions as their elders.

Revival Time

In 1998, *USA Weekend* got a surprising answer when it asked young people to rank the most important influences in their lives. Religion ranked second, behind parents but ahead of friends, peers, entertainers, teachers, and others. Two years later, a Gallup Youth Survey found that 94 percent of teenage respondents believed in God. Gallup researchers also found that more teenagers were worshipping than adults. In 2003, 43 percent of teenagers who responded to a Gallup Youth Survey said they attended religious services during the week prior to the poll. A similar Gallup survey taken that year found that 43 percent of adults also attended religious services during the prior week.

How can this phenomenon be explained? According to Neil Howe and William Strauss, authors of the book *Millennials Rising*, young people today seek comfort in the structure of the rituals and values offered by organized religion. They

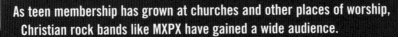
As teen membership has grown at churches and other places of worship, Christian rock bands like MXPX have gained a wide audience.

explain that "millennials"—children born after 1982 and before 2000—are the first generation to have been raised in a culture of protection.

As infants, these young people rode in legally mandated car seats with "Baby on Board" tags dangling from the window. As toddlers, their days were structured and organized in day-care centers. As children, they played in sports leagues after school and on weekends, chauffeured to games and practices by their "soccer moms." As adolescents, young people continue to search for structure through their faiths. Says Strauss, "For millennials, it's an organized thing. They're used to organized things—organized soccer, organized tests."

Christina Striebich, a 17-year-old Hawaiian, finds the structure she needs at her Greek Orthodox parish. She volunteers at the church, baking Greek pastries for fund-raising events. "Personally, I like the way it is orderly and traditional," Christina told a news reporter. "I like knowing what's going on, not feeling lost or not knowing what's going to happen in the future. It's comforting and reassuring."

Another researcher, Wade Clark Roof, reports that a large segment of teens is searching for that type of structure because it is not there in the home. He believes that many of these young people are growing up in broken families. Roof, who is professor of religion and society at the University of California, Santa Barbara, says: "Where the youth movements of the 1960s and 1970s were liberationist, movements are now constrictive, all about setting limits. There is a hunger for guidelines that parents haven't offered."

Conrad Cherry, an editor for the academic journal *Religion and American Culture* at Indiana University-Purdue University, considers the way today's teenagers have embraced their faiths to be very significant. In his view, the millennial generation is in the midst of a religious revival that shows itself in school prayer group membership and the popularity of Christian music acts such as the Newsboys, MXPX, Bebo Norman, Third Day, and P.O.D.

Instead of embracing every facet of their faiths, some teens are latching on to what they value the most. Ashling Gabig, a teenager living in Los Angeles, is being raised Catholic and educated in Catholic schools, yet she admits to having nontraditional views. "My perceptions of God and religion are quite different from those of a devout Catholic," she told a reporter. "I don't think of the pope as a holy man who is closest to God. I believe in Darwin's theory of evolution, and the possibility of God being a woman. I never believed in the story of Adam and Eve, because it was so demeaning towards women."

A Gallup Youth Survey published in November 2000 revealed that 58 percent of teenagers agreed that there is another religion besides their own that offers a path to God. Among the 500 respondents, 64 percent of the Catholics and 56 percent of the Protestants agreed with this statement. Also, the number of teenagers who describe themselves as "born again" is declining, according to Barna Research Group, a Ventura, California–based marketing firm that specializes in tracking cultural trends relating to the Church. Barna defined a born-again Christian as someone who has "made a personal commitment to Jesus Christ that is still important in [his or her] life today." In 1995, 10 percent of teens surveyed described themselves as evangelical. In 2002, that number had fallen to 4 percent.

As poll numbers reflect, some young people have sought out churches and synagogues in which they feel most comfortable, instead of settling for ones mom and dad pick out for the family. Houston, Texas, teenager Katie Beard and her parents are members of the First Presbyterian Church. Katie found the church for the Beards, who had previously attended a Baptist church. She told a reporter that having a strong belief system helped her put her life in perspective. "The stronger I grow in my faith, the more I realize I don't need to become a doctor or a lawyer or a brain surgeon and get large amounts of money to be happy in life," she said.

Turning to Faith

The structure that places of worship offer teens can be an alternative to many social ills that threaten their futures and even their physical safety and well-being. Underage drinking, pregnancy, sexually transmitted diseases, drug use, and violence are just some of the problems that teens face. To overcome those threats, a priest, pastor, rabbi, imam, or other spiritual leader may provide the right guidance.

Lynn Mitchell, religion scholar at the University of Houston, says the revival teens are experiencing may be a reaction against spiritual apathy and the typical self-destructive behavior of many teens. William Damon, director of the Stanford Center on Adolescence, agrees that religion has a tremendous affect on young people's lives. "There aren't a lot of positive things that predict avoiding risk—not IQ, where you live, all that stuff," he said. "Religion is one of the few positive

Religious youth groups provide teens the opportunity to share their faith with each other, as well as avoid situations in which they could use drugs and alcohol or engage in other risky behaviors.

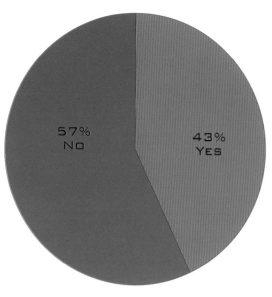

◀ Did you attend church or synagogue in the last seven days?

57%
No

43%
Yes

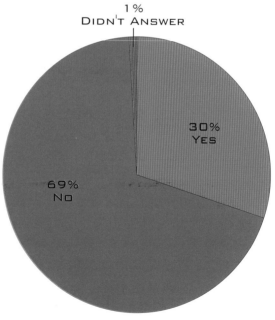

1%
DIDN'T ANSWER

30%
Yes

69%
No

▶ Did you take part in religious activites other than church or synagogue services in the last seven days, such as youth group meetings, religion classes, or choir rehearsals?

Poll taken August 2003; 517 total respondents.
Source: Gallup Youth Survey; The Gallup Organization

things you can add to a child's life."

Studies have shown that teens who rank their religious life highly are more likely to avoid harmful behaviors such as drinking, smoking, and having sex. For many teens, there are religious figures who serve as constant reminders of how individuals should conduct themselves. Joey Harper, a Christian living in Louisiana, says: "Everyone's tempted—go out, get drunk, get arrested. But if you think, 'Who would Jesus hang around with?'—it helps put it in perspective."

In a report issued in 2002, the nonprofit research organization Child Trends concluded that teenagers who are regular churchgoers often delay having sex until they are older. They are also less likely to partake of alcohol, marijuana, barbiturates, and cocaine; and they are less likely than non-religious teens to steal, destroy other people's property, and exhibit violent behavior.

University of Pennsylvania researchers Byron Johnson and Marc Siegel conducted a study of 2,358 poor black teenagers in Boston, Chicago, and Philadelphia in 2003. They concluded that teenagers who attend church every week are less likely to become involved in crime. In a separate study, University of Pennsylvania fellow John Wallace studied a cross-section of 4,000 high school seniors. Those who said they attend weekly services were half as likely to smoke, drink, and use marijuana as teens who do not spend time in church.

A September 2001 survey by the National Campaign to Prevent Teen Pregnancy polled 502 teens on the factors that influence whether or not they will have sex. Thirty-nine percent of the teens said their moral and religious beliefs had more impact on their sexual decisions than their fear of getting pregnant or contracting a sexually transmitted disease. Why do teenagers who go to church often avoid having casual sex, consuming alcohol and drugs, and other destructive types of behavior? Perhaps the answer can be found in the lessons that religions have been teaching for hundreds, and in some cases, thousands of years.

As it is recorded in the Book of Exodus in the Bible and in the Torah, the Prophet Moses came down from Mount Sinai after communing with God. Cradling two stone tablets in his arms, he delivered a set of ten laws that form the basis of Judeo-Christian values. The Ten Commandments admonish God's people not to lie, cheat, steal, murder, commit adultery, or worship other gods. They state that there is only one god, and that his name should not be taken in vain. Godly people must also remember the Sabbath day, respect their mother and father, and not plot against their neighbors.

During nearly every Christian or Jewish service, chances are good that at least one of God's commandments will be discussed, interpreted, or explained. The commandments bear a strong message that was meant to last for eternity. What's more, many of the nations on Earth have incorporated the commandments into their body of civil laws. Says Reverend Ted Haggard, president of the National Association of Evangelicals: "A lot of the ideas that underpin civil liberties come from Judeo-Christian theology."

How do spiritual commandments and other teachings get through to young people? Recently, it has occurred through more nontraditional ways than traditional ones. In 2002, a Gallup Youth Survey reported that 84 percent of the young people who said they had attended church in the week prior to the poll could recall the delivery of the sermon, but 55 percent couldn't recall the sermon's message. "[M]ost kids tune out most sermons—they don't want theological jargon, they want the message in a language they can understand," says Dr. Al Winseman, a United Methodist minister and consultant to the Gallup Organization.

Rather than getting the message from the pulpit, Winseman says, young people much prefer to be presented ideas in an interactive, group-oriented format. In other words, they don't want an adult preaching to them, which they most likely get too much of in school or at home. "[T]oday's teens are not a 'sit and listen' generation," says Winseman. "They need to participate."

Out of a desire to get involved, many teens have joined religious youth groups. In a 2003 Gallup Youth

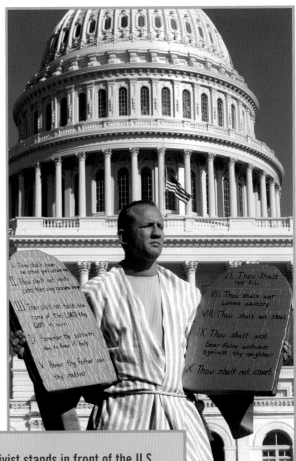

Dressed as the Prophet Moses, a Christian activist stands in front of the U.S. Capitol in Washington, D.C., to protest the ban on the public display of the Ten Commandments. The commandments are the basis for most Judeo-Christian morals.

Survey, 96 percent of 13- to 17-year-olds said they attended a youth group, religion class, or choir rehearsal at a church or synagogue during the previous seven days. The survey also asked those teens whether they had consumed alcoholic beverages dur-

IT'S COOL TO VOLUNTEER

So often those who serve the less fortunate have had their own experience with suffering. In the midst of facing a rare form of childhood cancer, Savannah Solomon gained compassion for the suffering of other young people, particularly those who undergo the isolating experience of chemotherapy treatment. In 2003, the year she was named valedictorian of Sandy Creek High School in Georgia, Solomon received an award for developing a project called "Red Carpet Day." The event was designed to give teenagers like her an enjoyable day at a concert or an amusement park.

Through Solomon's initiative, the Red Carpet Day project was able to offer 200 amusement park admission tickets to ill teenagers and their families living in the southern United States. Social workers at 13 hospitals were asked to select 2 adults and 12 teenagers for an all-expenses paid trip to Atlanta. Solomon asked that priority be given to teenagers who had suffered a cancer relapse or who had been confined to their homes.

While Solomon's project is unique, her example is not. Motivated by their compassion, which may stem from religious beliefs, many teens volunteer to help in homeless shelters, fire stations, nursing homes, and ambulance corps. A Gallup Youth Survey of 13- to 17-year-olds, conducted from April to June 2000, indicates that nearly half of all teenagers volunteer. In addition, more than half the teens who participated in the survey thought it would be a good idea for all young people to spend a year helping their communities or serving in the military.

Another Gallup survey, conducted between January and February

ing that period: 12 percent of the teens who did attend a service and 19 percent who didn't attend said they had consumed alcohol. Just 8 percent who said they were members of the youth group, a religion class, or the choir said they had been drinking.

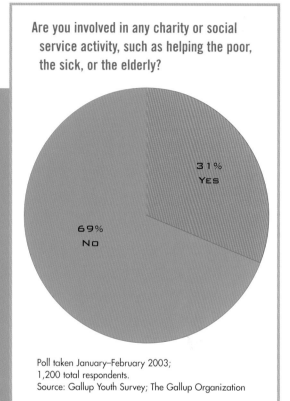

Are you involved in any charity or social service activity, such as helping the poor, the sick, or the elderly?

31%
YES

69%
No

Poll taken January–February 2003;
1,200 total respondents.
Source: Gallup Youth Survey; The Gallup Organization

2003, found that teens most likely to volunteer are those who perform at an above-average level in school and have parents who are college graduates. In addition, out of 1,200 respondents, 41 percent who regularly attend church volunteer—compared to the 25 percent of teens who do not regularly attend services.

As reported by Tom Culbertson, president of the volunteer organization Youth Services America, teens spent 2.4 billion hours of their time helping their communities in 1999. The U.S. Department of Education also reported that 64 percent of public schools, of which 83 percent were high schools, made community service programs available to their students that year.

During the hours when many teenagers are volunteering, they are avoiding opportunities to engage in risky activities like taking drugs. According to Search Institute, a Minneapolis-based organization that performs youth surveys for schools and communities, teens who volunteer just one hour a week are half as likely to abuse drugs, alcohol, and cigarettes.

David Knight, a Unitarian youth pastor, says church youth groups are valuable because they generally do not stifle the ideas of teenagers: "Youth fellowship groups, in particular, are a good place for teens to test out all the risk behaviors associated with coming of age. The fact that they *choose* to attend creates a sense of openness to receive the information in a new way." Adds George Barna, head of Barna Research Group:

> Teens do not go to youth groups for music and games, and they will not attend "adult church" for music and preaching. They demand transcendent adventures and supportive relationships. They need an outlet for their desire to have a positive effect on the world and to synchronize their inner drive to be needed with the needs of those in the world that have little.

Rachel Foster, who is Jewish and lives in Houston, credits a youth group at her synagogue with restoring her interest in Judaism when she reached high school age. A new youth director at her synagogue, Congregation Beth Am, began the youth group and Foster thought she would give it a try. She was surprised at how much West Houston United Synagogue Youth came to mean to her. She said, "It's become one of the most important things in my life. It's a place where I feel like I'm not the only one who wants to find out about why I'm Jewish and what it means to my life. It's always a place to turn to. Whenever I have a question, my religion has an answer for me." Religious leaders say churches and synagogues ought always to reach out to young people, and one of the best ways to do this is to organize youth groups and similar activities that allow teens to participate and do not smother them with preaching.

Religion and Universal Values

For those teens who do find comfort sitting in a church pew, though, there are many issues they must resolve for themselves.

Should young people be permitted to pray in school? Should creationism be taught in the same class that teaches the theory of evolution? Has a popular culture that often makes a hero of the bad guy prompted many teens to lie, cheat, and steal? Why do Muslims, Jews, and members of other religious groups face discrimination and hostility in the United States? What are the questions that face young people who grow up in mixed marriages? To the answers to these complicated questions, many spiritually minded people remained focus on the values of their faiths for guidance.

The values shared by Christians and Jews are not restricted to the Ten Commandments. Certainly, the New Testament and the rest of the Torah contain many lessons that young people can learn and use to mold their lives. Followers of the other major faiths learn similar values as well. Like believers of the monotheistic faiths of Christianity, Judaism, and Islam, Hindus believe in one Supreme Being, although that being assumes many different forms in gods and goddesses. Hindus also believe that all life is sacred and should be loved and revered. Thus, they highly esteem a life based on nonviolence, and advocate showing tolerance toward other religions.

Buddhists share similar beliefs, and their "Five Moral Precepts" are similar to the Ten Commandments in some ways. These precepts teach Buddhists to be nonviolent; to respect the property of others; to be faithful to one's spouse and other family members; to be honest; and to take care of one's own body, refraining from gluttony or the abuse of intoxicants.

The Qur'an (or Koran), the book Muslims believe to be the direct word of God as revealed to the Prophet Muhammad, entails many laws and lessons that guide young Muslims. One of the five basic rules, or pillars, of Islam is to recite a prayer of faith, known as *shahada* ("testimony"). This states, "There is no god but Allah, and Muhammad is His Prophet." Muslims are also required to give to charity, pray five times a day, fast during the holy month of Ramadan, and make at least one pilgrimage to Mecca in Saudi Arabia if they are capable.

Finding Religious Unity

Who among American teenagers are more likely to say that religion is important in their lives? According to the Gallup research, girls and African Americans. While 38 percent of young women told the researchers that religious faith was the most important influence in their life, only 28 percent of boys gave that response. Fifty-two percent of black teenagers rated religion as their most significant influence, while 29 percent of white teens gave religion that status. Geography also plays a role in the religious beliefs of American teenagers: Gallup researchers found that teens living in the South voiced a greater religious feeling than teens from other parts of the country.

RELIGIOUS AFFILIATIONS

Because the U.S. Census does not ask people their religious affiliations, there are no official estimates on adolescents regarding this subject. However, Gallup researchers and other experts have reported their own poll results. In 1999, two-thirds of Gallup teen respondents reported being a member of a church, synagogue, or organized religious group, and nearly half said they had attended services during the previous week. One-half was Protestant and one-quarter was Catholic. Ten percent was listed in a non-defined category.

Experts have found that the youths of this generation are increasingly more tolerant—and more curious—about religions

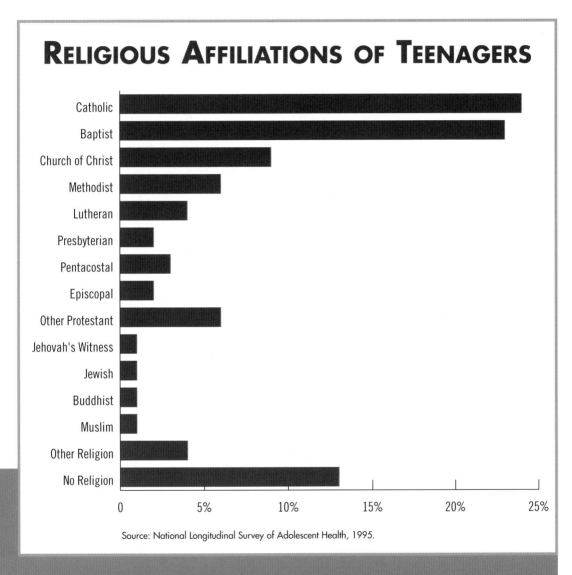

RELIGIOUS AFFILIATIONS OF TEENAGERS

Source: National Longitudinal Survey of Adolescent Health, 1995.

In 1995, the National Longitudinal Survey of Adolescent Health, a project of the University of North Carolina at Chapel Hill, also sought to determine how young believers between the ages of 13 and 18 classify themselves. The above graph is a breakdown of these teens and their faiths.

other than their own. As part of a special program, 17-year-old Teresita Boggess, a Catholic, had an opportunity to spend time with Jews, Muslims, Baha'is (followers of a religion advocating international unity), and other Christians her age. The program was sponsored by the San Diego office of the National Conference for Community and Justice, founded by a group of Christians and Jews seeking to promote tolerance. The participants were asked to attend ceremonies at different places of worship, then reconvene and discuss their impressions.

Prior to the program, Boggess had never given much thought to those who practiced other religions. She told a news reporter, "I just never had a clue what to think about them. But now I know they're just like me. Everyone in my group, we all decided we're going to meet and hang at our mall."

Aimal Laiq, a Baha'i, learned a lot from his first visit to a synagogue. "I knew nothing about the Jews, it was great," he said. "I got to know lots of things about the Jewish religion and how the system works." Since Baha'is preach tolerance and maintain that Abraham, Krishna, Moses, Jesus, and Buddha were all God's messengers, Laiq was familiar with this kind of activity. As a Christian, Tiffany Turner was less familiar with investigating other faiths, though she found it to be valuable experience. She was most taken with the worship she observed at a mosque. "That was so nice," she said. "I was touched about how they respected everything. They took off their shoes and everybody prays at the same time."

First-hand exposure to other religions is one of the best ways to rid oneself of preconceived notions. Scott Fox, another participant in the program, observed how this open discussion often directly leads to feelings of tolerance. The Jewish teen said, "It

kind of educated me that regardless of what I believe or someone else believes, that the only way that you can bring peace
through the world is through talking, talking to other people."
Scott's new Muslim friend, Saba Michael, agreed: "If we can
unite and have an understanding of each other, I think it's one
step closer to a peaceful world."

Chapter Three

The debate between Americans who want prayer in school and those who wish to preserve the separation of church and state is one of the longest standing clashes in public education.

Church and State: A Delicate Balance

In 1956, Ellory Schempp was excelling as an honor student, a member of the track team, and an active participant in his church's youth group. He was not the kind of student teachers expected would need discipline, but Eugene Stuhl, principal of Abington High School in suburban Philadelphia, became furious with the student one Monday morning.

Ellory had done the unthinkable. During morning prayers, at that time a typical activity at public schools in Pennsylvania, he had refused to stand when everyone else did. Instead he remained seated and read the Qur'an. Ellory's homeroom teacher was taken aback and sent him to the principal's office. No one had ever refused to participate in the morning Bible reading.

Ellory was a member of the Unitarian Church, a Protestant denomination that encourages its members to be tolerant of different interpretations of the Bible. Unitarians also believe in social justice and

OPINIONS ON PRAYER IN SCHOOL

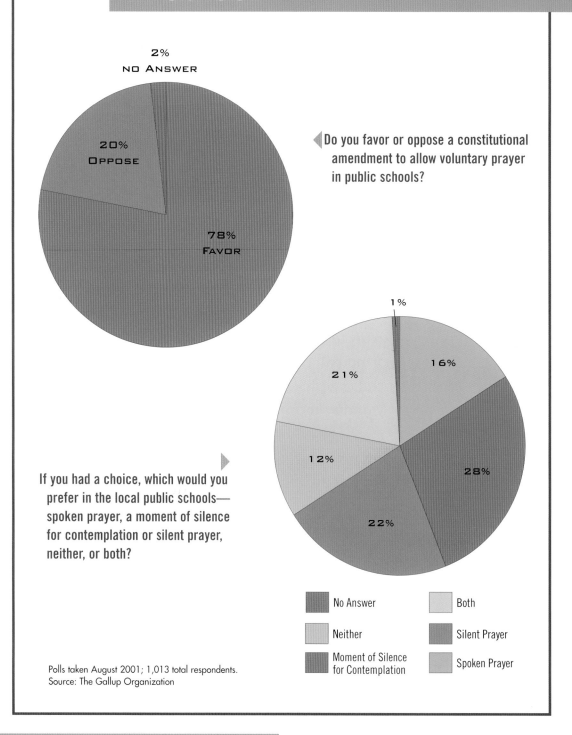

2%
NO ANSWER

20%
OPPOSE

78%
FAVOR

◀ Do you favor or oppose a constitutional amendment to allow voluntary prayer in public schools?

1%

16%

21%

28%

12%

22%

▶ If you had a choice, which would you prefer in the local public schools— spoken prayer, a moment of silence for contemplation or silent prayer, neither, or both?

	No Answer		Both
	Neither		Silent Prayer
	Moment of Silence for Contemplation		Spoken Prayer

Polls taken August 2001; 1,013 total respondents.
Source: The Gallup Organization

defending the rights of individuals. Ellory was familiar with the U.S. Constitution and was certain that the state's law requiring public school students to read from the Bible was contrary to the First Amendment, specifically its clauses regarding the separation of church and state. The amendment states:

> Congress shall make no law respecting an establishment of religion, or prohibiting the free exercise thereof; or abridging the freedom of speech, or of the press; or the right of the people peaceably to assemble, and to petition the Government for a redress of grievances.

Ellory wrote a letter to the American Civil Liberties Union, a nonprofit organization with a large staff of lawyers who defend people's civil rights. The ACLU agreed to help Ellory challenge the state law, but by the time the case was listed on the court's docket, Ellory had already entered college. His brother and sister took his place as plaintiffs in the lawsuit. In September 1958, the court ruled in favor of the Schempps and declared the Pennsylvania law unconstitutional.

The court ruling drew a great deal attention to the Schempp family. They received thousands of letters applauding their actions, while others took them to task. The two younger children were tormented by some of their classmates. The school district appealed the 1958 verdict and the case eventually made its way to the U.S. Supreme Court, where it was paired with another case challenging Maryland's mandatory school prayer law. That case was filed by an atheist named Madalyn Murray O'Hair on behalf of her son William.

On June 17, 1963, the Supreme Court outlawed government-sponsored, teacher-led prayer in schools. In his majority opinion, Supreme Court Justice William Brennan wrote, "It should be unnecessary to observe that our holding does not declare that the First

Amendment manifests hostility to the practice or teaching of religion, but only applies prohibitions incorporated in the Bill of Rights in recognition of historic needs shared by Church and State alike."

Abington v. Schempp became one of several landmark rulings and a precedent for future rulings regarding the separation of church and state. Reaction to the Supreme Court decision was mixed, however. Billy Graham, a popular evangelist, said, "At a time when moral decadence is evident on every hand, when race tension is mounting, when the threat of communism is growing, when terrifying new weapons of destruction are being created, we need more religion, not less."

Throughout the history of the U.S. education system, young people have been saying silent prayers to themselves at different points of the school day, such as the period before classes or the moments before an important test. The Equal Access Act, passed in 1984, states that these prayers are permissible, as long as they are not disruptive to other students. Students may also say grace in the cafeteria, read from their Bibles, and express their religious beliefs in their homework, artwork, or oral assignments.

In recent decades, many administrators have sought to extend these religious freedoms of students. There have been various attempts to re-institute prayer in schools, including several unsuccessful tries to add a school prayer amendment to the Constitution. Author Robert S. Alley, an authority on religious freedom, explains in his book *School Prayer* that during a period of 30 years, interest groups and politicians have legislated "to incorporate in . . . classrooms everything from prayer, to voluntary prayer, to silent prayer, to silent meditation or prayer, to a moment of silence."

Virginia legislators remained dedicated to maintaining some kind of meditation, even if it was not explicitly called prayer. In

2000, the state passed a law requiring that one minute of every day at a public school be set aside for such an activity. Children were required to sit quietly during that minute. High school student Emily Lesk viewed the new law as a blatant attempt to restore prayer to the school day. To show her opposition, she regularly walked out of the classroom during the minute of silence, and explained her actions in an essay published in *Newsweek* in 2001. She wrote:

> My opposition to this law is ironic because I consider myself religious and patriotic. I recite the Pledge of Allegiance daily (including the "one nation under God" part, which to me has historical, not religious implications). As a Reform Jew, I get peace and self-assurance from religious worship and meditation, both at my synagogue and in my home. But my religious education also taught me the importance of standing up against discrimination and persecution. . . . I've come to realize that taking a stand is about knowing why I believe what I do and refusing to give in despite the lack of support.

Lesk said she was often accompanied by about two dozen fellow students who would walk out with her. Even though she was aware that many other students disapproved of her action, she said that she felt "an obligation to act on behalf of the students all over Virginia who found their own beliefs violated but don't attend schools that allow them to express their opinions." She had hoped the Virginia law could be successfully challenged in court. The ACLU, which brought the suit, argued that the minute of silence was a thinly disguised method for encouraging school prayer, but in 2001, the U.S. Supreme Court refused to address the claim.

Religious Meetings in School

While a series of court cases have fleshed out what is and what is not acceptable to enforce regarding religious expression, violations occasionally still occur. In 1997, it was reported that Nitro High School in West Virginia used its public address system to

Before game time, football players gather to pray in the middle of the field at a Texas high school. The U.S. Supreme Court has allowed prayer sessions to take place as long as participation is not required.

offer prayers for the success of the school's football team. "They say it's illegal, but we've always done it," Athletic Director Patrick Vance explained to a reporter.

That same year in Pike County, Alabama, the parents of four Jewish children brought a lawsuit against their school district, accusing it of violating the children's religious freedoms. The suit stated that the family's seventh-grade daughter was made to bow her head for a student-led prayer, and the ninth-grade son was required by his vice principal to write an essay entitled "Why Jesus Loves Me" as a punishment for misbehaving. He was also forbidden to wear a Star of David, the symbol of Judaism, because his principal considered it a "gang symbol."

Few teenagers voice support for an oppressive policy such as this one, but according to a Gallup Youth Survey released in January 2001, teens do favor some aspects of religion in schools. Eighty-one percent of teens surveyed thought it is a good idea to make public school facilities available for religious groups' after-school meetings. Such a practice is allowed under the Equal Access Act.

Also included in the act is a clause allowing teachers of literature, history, and social studies to cover the Bible in their classes. It is a subject that 64 percent of teens stated should be included in their school curriculum. Claudia Wehmann, an English teacher at Mount Healthy High School in Cincinnati, Ohio, decided that the Bible need to be addressed more in her literature courses. She drew a surprised reaction from students when she developed a Bible and Literature elective course. Many wondered whether it was legal in a public school to teach a course that covered the Bible. Wehmann had the same concerns at first, before she discovered that both the American Civil Liberties Union and the National Council of Teachers of English support the teaching of such a course in public schools.

Conflicts over the Equal Access Act

The Equal Access Act requires that every federally funded secondary school that permits any interest club to meet must allow religious clubs to do the same, provided that there is no conflict with classes and the meetings are run by students who attend voluntarily. The act was challenged in 1990, only to be sustained by the Supreme Court by a vote of eight to one. President Bill Clinton, who supported the decision, said, "Nothing in the First Amendment converts our public schools into religion-free zones,

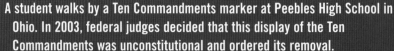

or requires all religious expression to be left behind at the schoolhouse door." Religious clubs are now a popular feature at high schools across the country, giving teens the chance to pray, interpret Bible verses, and hang out together. According to *Time* magazine, one out of four public schools had such a club in 1998.

During the administration of President George W. Bush, who took office in 2001, new controversies emerged over religion in school. In January 2002, Bush signed the No Child Left Behind federal education act, which affected the country's 90,000 public schools. The act was primarily an education reform measure, but it also announced that any school policy restricting students' rights of religious expression could result in the loss of federal funding.

Some concerned citizens opposed the government putting this

kind of pressure on schools. Barry Lynn, executive director of Americans United for the Separation of Church and State, said, "The 800-pound gorilla of these regulations is the threat of cutting off financial aid. The guidelines are so heavily weighted toward supporting alleged student-speech rights that schools will ignore legitimate concerns that a captive audience at graduation will be subjected to evangelism."

School prayer has been the subject of intense debate for years. With schools caught in the balance between granting freedoms of religious expression and maintaining the separation of church and state, it is likely that conflicts will continue to arise in the decades ahead.

Chapter Four

Biology teacher John Scopes (center) stands trial in 1925 for the charge of teaching Darwin's theory of evolution in the classroom. Even today, the clash between evolution and creationism in U.S. schools remains heated.

Evolution Challenged

In 1859, Charles Darwin introduced the world to his theory of evolution with the publication of *The Origin of Species*. The theory, which claims that every living thing on earth evolved over time through a process called natural selection, has since been embraced and explored by scientists, teachers, and students. Many religious people have rejected the theory, arguing that it refutes the Biblical account of how humans and the rest of the world were created. For decades these opponents, known as creationists, have railed against the teaching of evolutionary theory in public schools.

The majority of creationists are fundamental Christians. This group believes in a literal translation of the Bible—that the words in the Scriptures explicitly mean what they say and need no further interpretation. Typically, fundamentalists have conservative values: they believe in moral purity, personal accountability, and the sanctity of unborn life. They also believe there are long-established

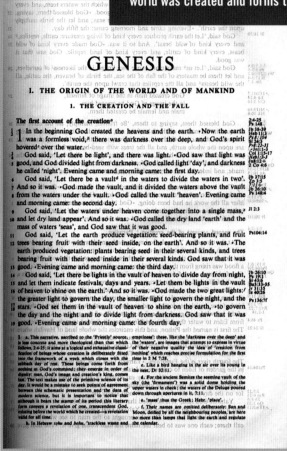

roles in society for men and women, and that the government has a right to legislate basic morals.

As for how the earth came to be populated by people, animals, and plants, creationists believe in the account presented in the Book of Genesis, in which God created all the world's plants and animals as they appear to us today. When people deny this account of creation, argue the creationists, they also deny God's divine plan. Some people have even linked teaching evolution in school to an overall decline in public morality. House Majority Leader Tom DeLay observed a link between the 1999 Columbine school shootings and the decline of modern culture, which in his estimation includes the teaching of evolution in schools. "Our school systems teach the children that they are nothing but glorified apes who are evolutionized out of some primordial soup," he said.

While some people find it difficult to reconcile their belief in God with evolution, for others Darwin's theory does not pose a threat to their faith. Pope Pius XII spoke favorably about evolution in 1950, and in 1996 Pope John Paul II made it clear that evolution was compatible with the Catholic Church's beliefs. The Episcopal, Presbyterian, United Methodist, and Evangelical Lutheran Churches are also receptive of evolution, as are a number of Jewish and Muslim sects.

Reverend Alfred Ruggiero of St. John's Lutheran Church in Pen Argyl, Pennsylvania, voices a sentiment shared by many progressive church leaders:

> I think evolution and a belief in God are completely compatible. Regardless of how I was formed, I have a relationship with God through Jesus Christ. . . . You don't go to the Bible for scientific facts, you go there for truth. God created the world and that's the truth. However that story is told, it doesn't necessarily affect the truth. I can certainly believe that God created the world, but I believe that God chose to do it through the evolutionary process.

The Scopes Trial

The most documented clash between evolutionists and creationists, the "Scopes Monkey Trial," took place in 1925 when a 25-year-old biology teacher named John Scopes stood trial for teaching evolution. At the urging of the ACLU, Scopes volunteered to test the constitutionality of the new Butler Act, which prohibited the teaching of evolution in his home state of Tennessee. The teacher and the ACLU anticipated they would lose the case, and then appeal to a higher court, where they ultimately hoped to see the law declared unconstitutional. Their plan was only partly successful. They lost the initial case, and Scopes was found guilty of violating the Butler Act and received a $100 fine.

But his conviction was overturned on a technicality, which prevented the case from being heard by a higher court.

Nonetheless, the trial captivated the minds of the nation and sparked debate about what should and should not be taught in school. It was also the subject of a popular play titled *Inherit the Wind*, written by Jerome Lawrence and Robert E. Lee in 1955. Later, the play was adapted into a movie starring Spencer Tracy, who won an Academy Award for his performance. Along with the controversial nature of evolutionary theory, what also made the trial so captivating were the celebrities who were involved. Scopes' defense attorney was Clarence Darrow, arguably the best courtroom tactician of the day. His opponent was William Jennings Bryan, a frequent candidate for the presidency. Both Darrow and Bryan were first-class orators and their courtroom theatrics made great copy for newspaper reporters.

While Scopes was the only defendant in the case, the clash between evolution and creationism really was the subject of the trial. The Scopes trial ruling temporarily closed the debate in the courtrooms, though it remained open in the court of public opinion. Only 2 of 15 other states considering bans on teaching evolution in the classroom adopted them. It took 43 years following the Scopes trial for the U.S. Supreme Court to hear another evolution case. In 1968, the court ruled that laws against teaching evolution violated the First Amendment. Yet even that ruling has not silenced the debate that continues in communities today.

Doug Linder, a professor of law at the University of Missouri in Kansas City, doesn't see the debate ending anytime soon. He said:

> Galileo was tried and convicted in 1632 for writing that the Earth revolved around the sun, rather than the other way around. It took the Vatican 200 years to remove Galileo's book from its list of banned books. That suggests to me that this debate could continue for a long time. I think that, to some

extent, evolution challenges the idea that we are special as a species, and that that is a difficult notion for many people, especially Christian fundamentalists, to accept.

In general, teenagers at least show an interest in creationism. A 1999 Gallup Youth Survey asked young people between the ages of 13 and 17 their opinions of evolution and creationism in the classroom. The survey found that 31 percent of the respondents thought evolutionary theory should be a required course, while 46 percent thought it should be an elective. These numbers mean that a total of 77 percent of the respondents believed evolution should be taught in school to some degree. But more teens endorse creationism as a school subject: 29 percent of the respondents believed creationism should be a required course while 60 percent thought it should be an elective, meaning that a total of 89 percent thought creationism has some place in the school curriculum.

Another Gallup Youth Survey conducted in 1999 found students to be of a similar mind about science and religion. When presented with a conflict between a scientific and religious explanation of something, 64 percent of teens said they would choose a religious explanation. Supporting this majority opinion is President George W. Bush, who has stated that he believes public school classes should discuss creationism along with evolution.

Many teens would no doubt agree with Michael Gray, a high school student in Georgia's Cobb County School District who took issue with his science curriculum. Gray told the Associated Press, "I had to do a term paper about evolution and there were just things that I could disprove or have alternate reasons for. I want my brother and sister to be given the option and not told it's the absolute truth." In response to the protests of parents and students like Gray, the school district unanimously agreed to allow teachers

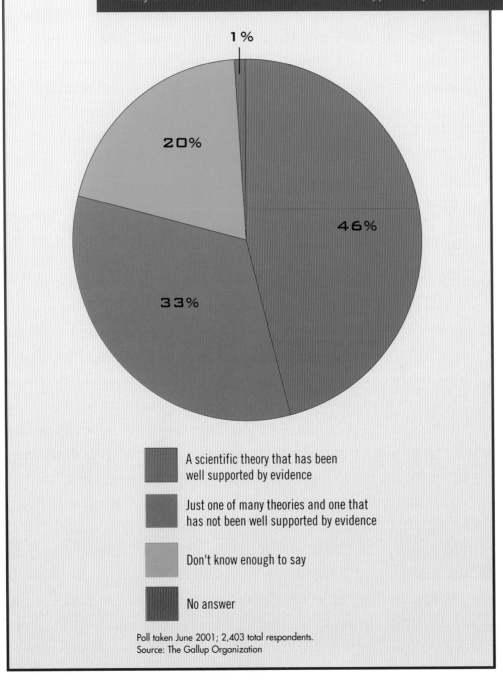

Do you think that Charles Darwin's theory of evolution is a scientific theory that has been well supported by evidence, or just one of the many theories and one that has not been well supported by evidence?

1%

20%

46%

33%

■ A scientific theory that has been well supported by evidence

■ Just one of many theories and one that has not been well supported by evidence

■ Don't know enough to say

■ No answer

Poll taken June 2001; 2,403 total respondents.
Source: The Gallup Organization

to discuss alternatives to evolution.

The debate over creationism in the Cobb County School District has been echoed in other parts of the country. The Kansas state legislature has grappled with the issue and has flip-flopped in its decisions. It first eliminated questions about evolution from statewide tests in 1999, and then brought them back in 2001. In the writing of their state assessment tests, Kentucky and Illinois use the less politically charged words "change over time" to describe evolution. Mississippi's high school biology tests make no mention of life's origins.

Alabamans have placed warning stickers on biology textbooks so students know that evolutionary theory is not above reproach. And in Pennsylvania, in the Souderton Area School District near Philadelphia, there was a heated debate in June 2003 over a new geography book and its references to an evolutionary progression between apes and humans. School board director Sharon Gehret, who opposed using the book in classrooms, pointed out, "It is stated in the book that we came from apes. Not as theory, as fact." She, too, wanted to place a sticker on the book over an illustration of hominids, whom scientists believe are early ape-like versions of human beings.

A group of parents supported Gehret. Chris French, who discovered that his daughter's biology textbook did not mention any other origin theories besides evolution, told a newspaper reporter, "The book was offensive to us as a family." But Sonnet Graham, a student at Souderton Area High School, expressed her disapproval of the sticker proposal, saying that high school students were old enough to decide what they wanted to believe without the school board acting as censors. In the end, the school board approved using the book by a vote of six to three.

Doug Linder, a law professor and expert who tracks the creationism agenda activity in the United States, reported that between 1999 and 2001, there were campaigns to include creationism in curricula in 28 states, in every region of the country but New England.

Intelligent Design

Recently, the battle between creationists and evolution proponents has begun a new chapter with the emergence of a new, more sophisticated counter-evolution theory called "intelligent design," first conceived by Dr. Michael J. Behe. A number of the theory's adherents are prominent scientists. In his book *Darwin's Black Box: The Biochemical Challenge to Evolution*, Behe pointed out what he believed were holes in Darwin's theory, in particular the flaws in his descriptions of cell structure development.

Unlike creationists, intelligent design proponents acknowledge that the world is billions of years old, but they still assert that it was designed by God or some other intelligent force. "The most striking thing about the intelligent design folks is their potential to really make anti-evolutionism intellectually respectable," said Dr. Eugenie Scott, executive director of the National Center for Science Education, a pro-evolution group.

Dr. Guillermo Gonzalez, an astronomer at the University of Washington in Seattle, thinks the design theory is plausible. He said, "I'm very impressed with the level of scientific work and the level of scientific dialogue among the leaders of the design movement." Other scientists are not as kind in their assessments. Dr. Leonard Krishtalka, director of the University of Kansas Natural History Museum and Biodiversity Research Center, says intelligent design is "nothing more than creationism dressed in a cheap tuxedo."

Design proponents have their own analogy, which Mark Edwards, spokesman for the Discovery Institute and Center for the Renewal of Science and Culture, finds more appropriate. They call themselves "punk rockers of evolutionary biology" because they make noise by challenging the established mode of thinking.

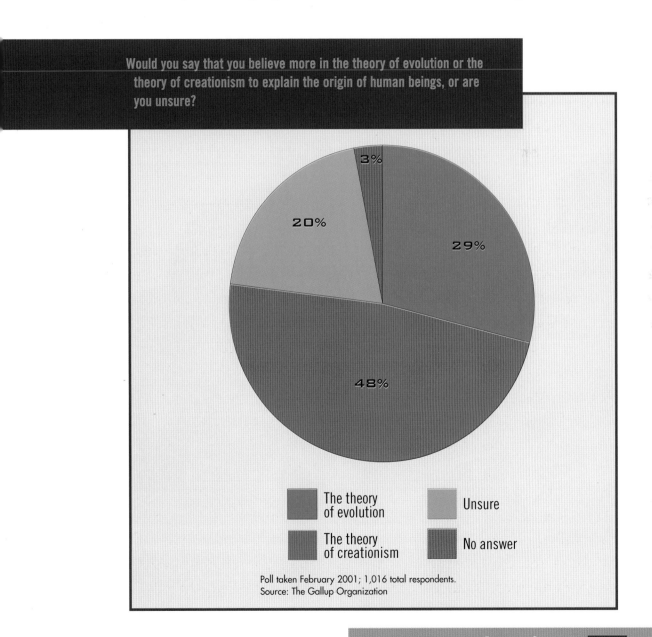

Would you say that you believe more in the theory of evolution or the theory of creationism to explain the origin of human beings, or are you unsure?

3%

20%

29%

48%

The theory of evolution

The theory of creationism

Unsure

No answer

Poll taken February 2001; 1,016 total respondents.
Source: The Gallup Organization

Chapter Five

Two Catholic girls cheer as they wait for the arrival of Pope John Paul II to the United States. In addition to revering the prominent figures of the major faiths, many teens embrace traditional beliefs and morals.

Here Come the Traditionalists

As teenagers, the baby boomers were much different than their children are today. Several decades ago, the Gallup Organization and other research groups chronicled the drug experimentation, rebelliousness, and sexual freedom of the baby boom generation, whose members were born in the years between 1946 and 1964. Researchers have found that today's teens are much more traditional than their parents were in their attitudes and their personal habits. They are less likely to use alcohol, tobacco, and marijuana than their parents, and less likely to approve of premarital sex or having children outside marriage.

Dr. George Gallup Jr., chairman of the Gallup Institute, notes that the millennials hold a number of conservative views. The teenagers of this generation "want to reduce the amount of violence on TV, seek clear rules to live by, and promote the teaching of values in school. They are searching eagerly for religious and spiritual moorings in their

Teens (aged 13–17) who attend church

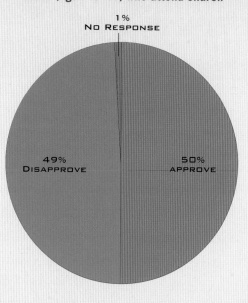

1%
NO RESPONSE

49%
DISAPPROVE

50%
APPROVE

Teens (aged 13–17) who do not attend church

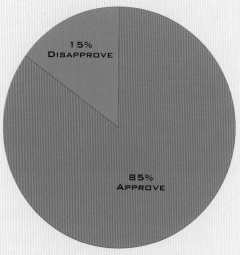

15%
DISAPPROVE

85%
APPROVE

Poll taken January–February 2003; 1,200 total respondents.
Source: Gallup Youth Survey; The Gallup Organization

lives. They want abstinence taught in school, and they think divorces should be harder to get."

Gallup research also shows that teens think their generation will be more tolerant of differing lifestyles, races, and sexual orientations and grow up to enjoy a world that is less polluted, more peaceful, and more caring. Ask teens who their role models are and the answers are fairly traditional, too. In a Gallup Youth Survey of 1,200 respondents aged 13 to 17, 11 percent of teens said their mother was the woman they admired most, while 7 percent chose their father as the man they admired most. The most admired man next to father was President George W. Bush, who was chosen by 6 percent of teens.

Losing the Slacker Image

According to the Barna Research Group, teenagers began feeling more satisfied in the mid-1990s, abandoning the "slacker" image that characterized members of Generation X, who reached adolescence in the 1980s. But if there is a dent in the image the millennials have of themselves, it is that four out of five teens believe that adults view them with distrust. Nonetheless, Barna Research reports that today's teens are no longer the angry, disengaged adolescents many adults imagine them to be. These teens have goals that are very similar to their parents' goals: they want a good education, strong relationships with other people, and a lifestyle that is as healthy as their parents'.

There is other evidence that today's teens embrace traditional beliefs. In 2000 the Gallup Youth Survey asked 500 teens if they believe in a judgment day, and if good people will go to heaven even if they do not believe in God. In a breakdown of the two major denominations, 88 percent of Protestants said there would

TEEN VIEWS ON ABORTION

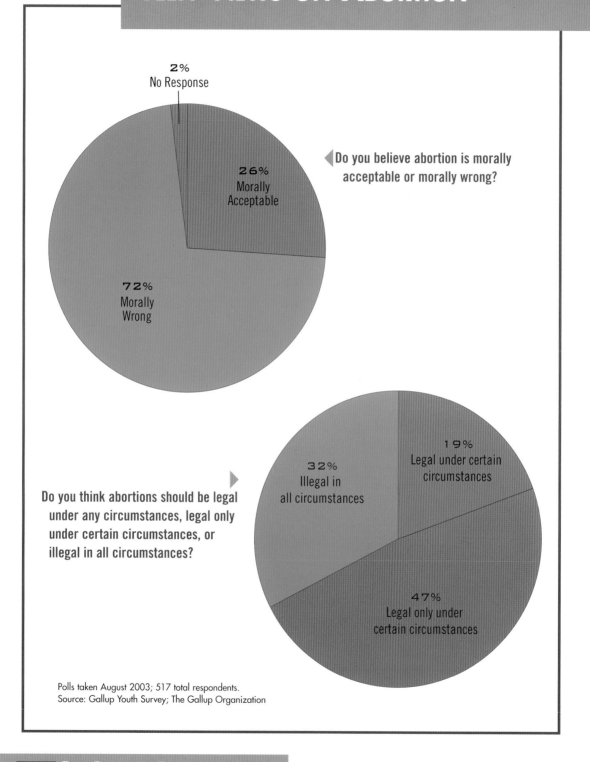

2%
No Response

26%
Morally
Acceptable

◀ Do you believe abortion is morally acceptable or morally wrong?

72%
Morally
Wrong

32%
Illegal in
all circumstances

19%
Legal under certain circumstances

▶ Do you think abortions should be legal under any circumstances, legal only under certain circumstances, or illegal in all circumstances?

47%
Legal only under
certain circumstances

Polls taken August 2003; 517 total respondents.
Source: Gallup Youth Survey; The Gallup Organization

be a judgment day and 81 percent of Catholic teens agreed. Thirty-seven percent of Protestant teens thought that someone might end up in heaven who did not believe in God, and 63 percent of Catholics thought it was not necessary to believe in God to go to heaven.

In the same survey, teens showed that they don't always agree with some of the religious morals to which they have been exposed. For example, 39 percent of teens (30 percent Protestant, 46 percent Catholic) said they don't believe in everything their religion teaches. In a study performed by the Fort Wayne, Indiana–based Christian Community Inc., a majority of the teens felt their congregations were not providing them with enough information about integrating faith with concerns about sex, marriage and parenting. Christian Community, which provides social research for Christian congregations, interviewed nearly 6,000 teenagers between 2000 and 2002.

Today, both adults and teenagers are using the Internet for a variety of purposes, including the discussion of religion. In a 2003 study done by Harris Interactive and Teenage Research Unlimited for the Internet search engine Yahoo!, people aged 13 to 24 were found to spend 16.7 hours per week on the Internet, three hours more than they spend watching television. Those polled said they enjoyed spending time on the Internet because unlike radio and television, it gives them the freedom to control the content.

Out of a group of 620 teens between the ages of 13 and 18, 16 percent told Barna Group researchers that they expected the Internet to replace their regular church within five years. Black teens were four times more likely to hold this view than white teens. Barna also said that 25 million adults are already using the

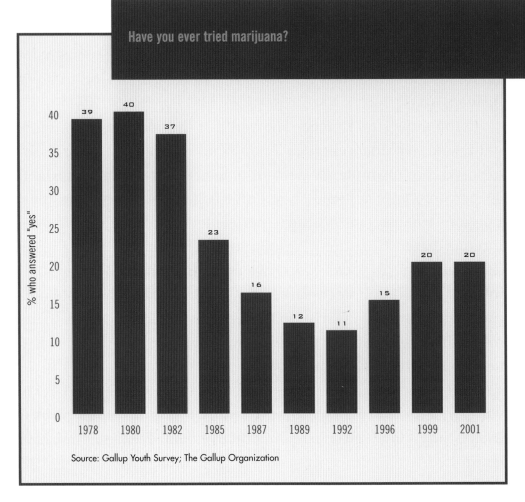

% who answered "yes"

40   39
      40
35   37
30
25   23
20
16
15   12   11   15   20   20
10
5
0

1978   1980   1982   1985   1987   1989   1992   1996   1999   2001

Source: Gallup Youth Survey; The Gallup Organization

Internet in their religious lives. Only about 4 percent of teens said they were using the Internet for religious purposes. Born-again Christians were among the leading groups of teenagers most likely to use the Internet for matters of faith. The company's president, George Barna, said:

> A large proportion of teenagers use the Net for conversation with others. A substantial number of cyberchatters engage in dialogue related to faith, spirituality, religion, meaning and truth—the very types of conversations that are often initiated or fostered by churches. Teens do not think of those conversations as religion expression, but the sense of community and the spiritual

beliefs fostered by such dialogue on spiritual matters is identical to what the traditional church seeks to create within its congregation. . . .

Barna also reported that his organization's research predicts that by 2010, 10 percent to 20 percent of the population will be "relying primarily or exclusively upon the Internet for its religious input." This population segment believes spiritual needs can be met in the home, which could mean a drop in church attendance nationwide.

Current research shows that more Americans are exploring their faith on the Internet through online discussions. With the growth of this population segment, church attendance could decrease in the coming decades.

Chapter Six

The moral codes of the church and other religious institutions sometimes protect teenagers from the temptation to cheat.

Surrendering
to Temptation

At 18, college freshman Luke Thompson seemed far ahead of his classmates. The Yardley, Pennsylvania, teen was running a bargain fare airline ticketing agency while attending Babson College in Wellesley, Massachusetts. He began the business as a freshman after developing a first-class Internet promotion and ticketing site. His Mainline Airways had been offering $89 fares from Honolulu to Los Angeles when the business hit some turbulence. His exceedingly low airfares had attracted the attention of the attorney general of Massachusetts, who filed a suit against the teen after determining Luke was operating a bogus airline with no fleet.

If Luke cheated the public, as the attorney general's office alleged, he may have been directly following in the footsteps of a slew of business executives whose transgressions made the newspapers in the first years of the 21st century. During that period executives of corporations like WorldCom,

Tyco, and Enron were charged with fraud and stealing money from investors and employees.

The United States, like many other countries, has a history of cheating. Teenage cheaters often have modeled their behaviors after adults. Why do people cheat? Americans have been wrestling with that question for some time.

A Short History of Cheating

In the world of sports, cheaters may resort to steroid use. The International Olympic Committee surveyed 2,200 athletes at 11 U.S. colleges and found that some 6 percent of males and 1 percent of females use steroids to enhance their performances. A steroid is a synthetic derivative of the male sex hormone testosterone. It helps create muscle mass, making an athlete stronger. A weightlifter using steroids can lift more weights; a sprinter can run faster; and a football lineman can capitalize on his added strength and bulk to become a better blocker.

Physicians may prescribe steroids for the purpose of treating patients who have lost muscle mass from diseases such as AIDS, but athletes use and abuse them to get a beat on the competition. Steroids have many dangerous side effects, including heart, liver, and kidney failure. In college and professional sports, athletes who are found to be using steroids are often suspended from competition. Nevertheless, college and professional athletes use steroids with the full knowledge that they can suffer life-threatening illnesses.

Americans haven't always found exemplary models in their political leaders, who have sometimes resorted to cheating themselves. In 1972, President Richard M. Nixon was on his way to winning re-election by a landslide. On the night of June 17, five men were arrested inside the headquarters of the Democratic National Committee in the Watergate Hotel in Washington, D.C. Police found the men in possession of electronic eavesdropping devices they intended to plant in the Democrats' offices. The public learned later that these men had been hired by President Nixon's campaign committee. In anticipation of the election that fall, they had been looking for information on the Democrats' plans. Nixon's aides hoped to exploit this information to give the president, a Republican, an advantage in the coming campaign.

The scandal that erupted following the arrest of the burglars became known as Watergate and led to the convictions of several top aides in the Nixon administration, as well as the resignation of the president himself in 1974. He resigned after it was revealed that he intended to use the resources of the federal government to launch a cover-up of the crime. In 2003, former Nixon aide Jeb Stuart Magruder told a national TV audience that he believed the president even had advance knowledge of the burglary itself.

Cheating is not limited to politics and government. Many other American institutions have been tarnished by cheating scandals. In the entertainment world, there was the scandal of the game show *Twenty-One*. Game shows had been popular on radio for years by the time television sets started finding their way into American homes in the 1950s. Soon, the shows made the transition to TV. *Twenty-One*, one of the most popular game shows, required contestants to answer a series of questions dealing with history, science, the arts, and other subjects for cash prizes.

The TV show's producers had found that viewers preferred some contestants over others, and in order to keep popular contestants coming back week after week, the producers began giving them the answers before airtime. In 1956, with the help of some presupplied answers, college student Herbert Stempel won the quiz for five straight weeks and collected nearly $50,000 in prize money, but then the producers brought in Columbia University English professor Charles Van Doren to challenge Stempel. The two men went head-to-head for four weeks; during that time, it became clear to the producers that Van Doren—an urbane, well-bred intellectual—was much more popular among viewers.

Armed with a set of answers, Van Doren beat Stempel, who was asked to throw the game. Van Doren went on to have a very popular run as a *Twenty-One* champion, collecting some $130,000 in prize money. The secret arrangement worked out very nicely until Stempel, fuming because he believed he could have beaten Van Doren in an honest head-to-head match, complained to the newspapers and disclosed that *Twenty-One* was fixed. A congressional committee held hearings on the show and exposed all the details of the scandal.

A few infamous journalists have been found to have cheated while making their way through the reporting ranks. In 1981, the *Washington Post* was forced to admit that one of its reporters, Janet Cooke, had concocted a story about an eight-year-old heroin addict named Jimmy. When it was published, Cooke's story sent shockwaves through Washington with its sordid tale of a young boy addicted to drugs. The story was so compelling that Cooke received the prestigious Pulitzer Prize for her reporting. Police searched through the Washington neighborhoods for the boy but were unable to find him, prompting local political leaders to question whether he truly existed. When Cooke admitted to making up the story, she lost her job and the newspaper was forced to return the Pulitzer Prize.

Teens and Cheating

Donald McCabe, a professor at Rutgers University and founder of the Center for Academic Integrity, points out that teenagers look to adults to provide them with their moral framework. When adolescents see adults practicing poor moral judgment, they don't understand why younger people should be held more accountable.

To be sure, the millennial generation has its share of cheaters. In a Gallup Youth Survey conducted in 2001, 73 percent of 13- to 17-year-olds admitted to lying occasionally; 53 percent of 16- and 17-year-olds confessed they had cheated on tests. The Gallup research said the number of teens cheating on exams has declined since 1981, when the figure was 66 percent.

If their moral compasses sometimes need adjusting, at least a majority of teens have old-fashioned guilt to keep them in line, according to study results. In a 2003 Gallup Youth Survey, 77 percent said they would feel guilty if they cheated on a test; 88 percent of teens said they would feel guilty if they stole; and 80 percent said they would feel disloyal if they betrayed their group of friends. The most guilt-prone teens were those who live in the suburbs.

Children of white-collar parents who attended college are more likely to cheat than their blue-collar peers. Forty-six percent of teens said there is a fair amount of cheating going on at their schools. Girls are more likely to admit to cheating than boys, and older teens are more likely to cheat than younger teens.

For many teenagers, their guilty feelings about lying, cheating, and similar transgressions may be attributed in some degree to the lessons of their religions. Catholics are encouraged to go to confession, where they sit down with a priest to confess their sins. In Judaism, the holiest time of the year is the 10-day period between the Jewish New Year, known as Rosh Hashanah, and the Day of Atonement, known as Yom Kippur. During this period, Jews are encouraged to ponder the wrongs they committed during the past year and find ways to atone for their sins.

Many Protestant denominations encourage members to give testimony — to address the congregation and talk about their lives before they found Christ. They also may admit to crimes or sins against their friends and family. Many church hymns contain lyrics celebrating the personal depths from which they have been brought, as in one of the faith's most popular hymns, "Amazing Grace":

> Amazing grace! How sweet the sound
> That saved a wretch like me!
> I once was lost, but now am found;
> Was blind, but now I see.

Still, teenagers often cannot avoid resisting certain temptations to cheat. Many of them feel pressure from their parents, teachers, and peers to excel. What may fuel the desire to cheat is the pressure to get good grades and participate in enough extracurricular activities so that they can win admission into selective colleges and universities. A Gallup Youth Survey conducted in the summer of 2000 found that only a little more than half of 13- to 17-year-olds thought that cheating on exams was a very serious matter. However, they had no trouble recognizing the serious nature of physically abusing someone, committing a hate crime, or engaging in prostitution.

Alice Newhall, who graduated from George Mason High School in Virginia, has made conclusions about the cheater's mindset. She told a reporter for CNN: "Cheating is a shortcut and it's a pretty efficient one in a lot of cases. . . . What's important is getting ahead. The better grades you have, the better school you get into, the better you're going to do in life. And if you learn to

CHEATING IN SCHOOLS

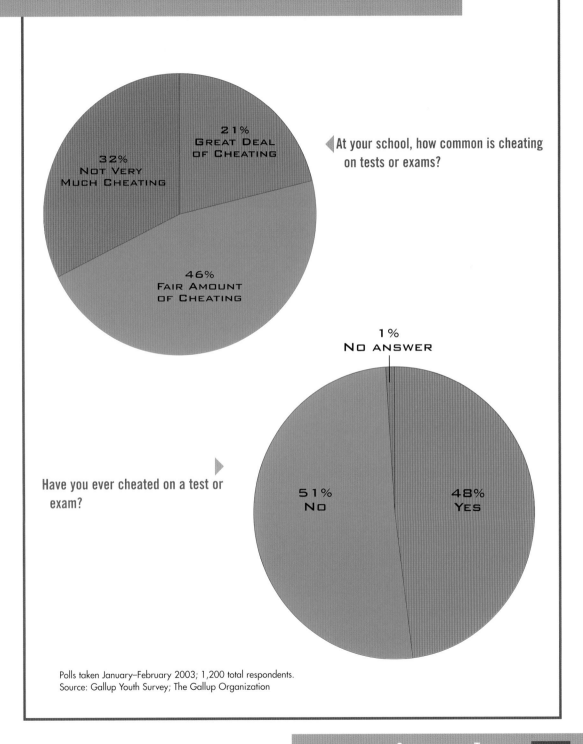

21%
GREAT DEAL
OF CHEATING

32%
NOT VERY
MUCH CHEATING

At your school, how common is cheating on tests or exams?

46%
FAIR AMOUNT
OF CHEATING

1%
NO ANSWER

Have you ever cheated on a test or exam?

51%
NO

48%
YES

Polls taken January–February 2003; 1,200 total respondents.
Source: Gallup Youth Survey; The Gallup Organization

WHAT TEENAGERS FEEL GUILTY ABOUT

	Total	Attended religious services in past week	Did not attend
Neglecting your parents when they are old	92%	95%	90%
Stealing something	88%	92%	86%
Not paying a debt	83%	84%	82%
Lying to a friend	81%	89%	75%
Being disloyal to your group	80%	84%	76%
Cheating on a test in school	77%	85%	70%
Surfing for pornography on the Internet	77%	85%	70%
Swearing or cursing at a teacher	75%	83%	69%
Having sexual intercourse before you are married	59%	79%	44%

Poll taken June–September 2001; 454 total respondents.
Source: The Gallup Organization

cut corners to do that, you're going to be saving yourself time and energy. In the real world, that's what's going to be going on. The better you do, that's what shows. It's not how moral you were in getting there."

Breaking the Honor Code

In 2000, *Newsweek* asked some teenagers to photograph what was important in their lives. Some of the teens used the opportunity to reflect on the pressure they felt to do well in school. Lauren Bogenschutz, a 17-year-old, took a picture of a mailbox as a reminder of her constant communication with colleges that might accept her. Kathryn Griffin, 18, submitted a photograph of herself at work on her computer. She wrote, "If I'm not at school or at work, I'm at home on my laptop, typing essays, looking up French words online or researching the information."

One common way that students cheat is through plagiarizing. Using someone else's work without proper attribution has become more common because of the Internet, though it has also become easier to spot with the emergence of watchdog web sites like Turnitin.com. Setting a poor example for teenagers, a number of prominent adult writers have been accused of lifting passages from other writers. Jayson Blair, formerly a *New York Times* reporter, the late historian Stephen Ambrose, and songwriter Bob Dylan are some of the most well-known cases. The *Boston Globe* even found examples of school administrators using unattributed material from other sources in their letters to parents.

In 2002, at a 450-student high school in Kansas, a case of widespread plagiarism made international headlines. Teacher Christine Pelton failed 28 of her 118 sophomore botany students at Piper High School for plagiarizing an assignment that was worth half their grades. The assignment, which involved collecting and analyzing leaves, had taken six months to complete and had been given by the school in years past. Pelton determined that the students, who had been warned not to plagiarize, "borrowed" information from a web site instead of writing their own observations as they were instructed. She confirmed her suspicions by using a database on Turnitin.com that determines if plagiarism has taken place.

When the parents of the 28 students learned about the failing grades on the assignment, many protested to the school board. In a meeting closed to the public, the school board asked the biology teacher to raise the students' grades, despite the proof they had seen that the teens had copied. Pelton, who was only in her second year of teaching, refused to alter the grades and resigned. At least one other teacher resigned, as did the school's principal.

Cheating is a problem on college campuses as well as in high schools. The Center for Academic Integrity monitored cheating in college classrooms for 10 years. During that period, the center interviewed more than 12,000 students at 40 U.S. colleges and universities, and learned that 5,600 of the 7,000 undergraduates interviewed at small to medium-sized colleges cheated at least once. Fraternity and sorority members were more likely to cheat than non-Greek students, and cheating occurred much less frequently on campuses where there was an honor code. One out of sixteen students admitted to cheating on campuses where there was an honor code, and one out of five students cheated on campuses that lacked such a code. The studies also found that many college professors don't turn in cheaters and that students quickly catch on to their instructors' lack of vigilance.

About 100 colleges and universities have honor codes that prohibit students from lying and cheating. Fellow students are asked to turn in code violators. The University of Virginia's honor code is unusually strict. Students found to be in violation are expelled and may forfeit their degrees. Harvard University has a similarly strict honor code. In the summer of 2003, New Jersey teenager Blair Hornstein saw her acceptance to Harvard withdrawn after the school discovered that she plagiarized portions of stories she had written for a local newspaper. Hornstein had violated

Harvard's honor code before setting foot in a classroom.

Many high schools have well-established plagiarism policies and educate their students about the do's and don'ts of writing academic research papers. Students generally value having these guidelines spelled out. In fact, honesty is one character trait that most teens agree should be taught in school. A 2001 Gallup Youth Survey found that 91 percent of teens participating in a Gallup Youth Survey agreed that schools should turn out honest students.

Chapter Seven

Teenagers of minority faiths have found ways to celebrate Western customs, like attending a school prom, without compromising the laws of their religion.

Growing up Muslim in the United States

Fatima Haque attended her high school prom in a silver gown that shimmered in the overhead strobe lights. That evening, the 18-year-old student from San Jose, California, danced the night away and said goodbye to her high school days. But Fatima didn't dance with any young men, because boys were not invited to this prom. In fact, the windows of the rented hall were covered to prevent boys from looking in.

Fatima and 16 of her Muslim friends attended a prom that was restricted to girls. This arrangement followed the strict tenets of Islamic law know as the Sharia. Under the code, dating, dancing, and having physical contact with males before marriage is forbidden. What's more, many Muslim girls are required to keep their bodies and heads covered. On the way to her prom, Fatima wore a shawl to cover her gown as well as a scarf known as a *hijab* to cover her head.

"These young women are being very creative,

finding a way to continue being Muslim in the American context," Jane I. Smith, a professor of Islamic studies, said of Fatima and her friends. "Before, young Muslims may have stuck with the traditions of their parents or rejected them totally to become completely Americanized. Now, they're blending them."

As Muslim Americans, Fatima and the others have learned they must use ingenuity to adapt to American ways and yet still be loyal to their Islamic upbringing. They are not alone. According to the City University of New York's American Religion Identification Survey (ARIS), there are about 1.4 million Muslims in the United States under the age of 18. The U.S. State Department reports that Muslim Americans, who number some 6 million, are members of the fastest-growing religious group in the country, and it predicts that by 2010 there will be more Muslims than Jews in the United States. The country's youth are very much a factor in this growth of Islam.

Many Muslim Americans, particularly teenagers, find sharp contrasts between what Islamic law permits them to do and what is regarded as acceptable behavior in American society. The Sharia spells out the moral goals of a community and applies to the religious, political, social, and private dimensions of a Muslim's life. It is based on the Qur'an as well as other sources like the *Sunna*, an early interpretation of the Qur'an written by Islamic scholars.

Typically, Muslim Americans have to make certain exceptions to the Sharia. For instance, it is rare to see a Muslim woman walking behind her husband on the street in the United States, as is common in Saudi Arabia or Afghanistan. Nevertheless, many Muslim American women keep their heads covered and also observe strict dietary laws. In most Muslim American homes, alcohol, tobacco, and illegal drugs are forbidden.

Adeel Iqbal, an 18-year-old high school student, knows something about the temptations Muslims feel when they are exposed to American culture. "Every day we're bombarded with images of sex and partying and getting drunk, in music and on TV, so of course there's a curiosity," he said. "When you see your own peers engaging in these activities, it's kind of weird. It takes a lot of strength not to participate. But that's how I've been raised. When your peers see you're different in a positive way, they respect it."

Muslim American teens who compete in sports may face physical demands during the holy month of Ramadan, when Muslims are required to fast.

Ramadan, the holiest month of the Islamic calendar, can be a challenging time for Muslim Americans. The month observes the time when the Qur'an was revealed to the Prophet Muhammad, the founder of the Islamic faith. During Ramadan, Muslims abstain from food and drink during the daylight hours and are encouraged to devote more time to meditation, strengthening their relationships, and studying the Qur'an.

For young Muslims trying to fit into American society, observing Ramadan also poses its challenges. For example, student athletes who must fast during the daytime often find themselves growing weary as they train or compete in rigorous sporting events. "Training with no water or food . . . it was difficult at times," Ahmed Haji, a cross-country star at a Connecticut high school, said of Ramadan.

More American schools are beginning to accommodate the religious needs of Muslim students, in a similar fashion to how they accommodate students of other faiths. Still, some Muslim American teens find themselves isolated. Hala Saadeh, a student at Fitchburg High School in Massachusetts, is the only Muslim among the school's 1,286 students. "I have friends there," she told a news reporter in 2002. "But there are so many things we just can't talk about. I actually have to go home and call friends in other cities to talk."

Elsewhere, young Muslim Americans find other ways to maintain their heritage while remaining a part of American society. On college campuses, for example, many Muslim American students design their schedules to avoid having classes on Friday afternoons, a time Muslims reserve for a traditional congregational prayer known as *Jum'aa*. Some colleges have responded to the needs of their Muslim students by hiring religious leaders, known as imams, to lead Muslim prayer services, and by setting aside campus facilities to serve as makeshift mosques.

Prejudice Against Muslims

Many young Muslim Americans have risen to the challenge of assimilating to life in the United States. Still, there is no denying that in the years after the September 2001 terrorist attacks, which were orchestrated by Islamic fundamentalists, prejudice against Muslims has become more common. In a 2003 Gallup Youth Survey, 29 percent of 13- to 17-year-olds admitted they would feel uncomfortable having a Muslim as their roommate. Another Gallup Youth Survey conducted later in the year reported that many young American teens harbor a prejudice against Muslims, despite their lack of knowledge about the Islamic faith.

In the same survey, just 28 percent of the respondents said they know Muslims. Forty-five percent said they have been exposed to education or have held discussions about Islam in their schools. The poll was taken in August 2003, during a period in which positive relations between Muslims and Americans of other faiths were especially threatened. American troops stationed in Iraq — a predominantly Muslim country — found themselves under fire by Iraqi insurgents loyal to dictator Saddam Hussein, deposed just three months earlier. Each day, the headlines reported U.S. soldiers killed in surprise attacks by Islamic terrorists and guerrillas.

In the Gallup survey, when young respondents were asked if they agree or disagree with the statement "Most Muslims around the world want peace," 30 percent disagreed. Just 46 percent of young people agreed that "most Muslims around the world are

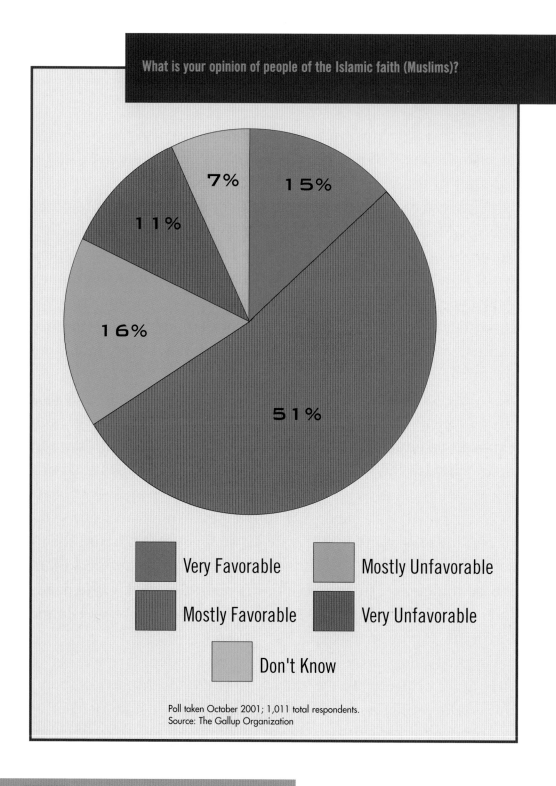

What is your opinion of people of the Islamic faith (Muslims)?

7%

15%

11%

16%

51%

Very Favorable   Mostly Unfavorable

Mostly Favorable   Very Unfavorable

Don't Know

Poll taken October 2001; 1,011 total respondents.
Source: The Gallup Organization

accepting of other races," and just 34 percent said that "most Muslims around the world are accepting of other religions."

Young Muslim Americans experience the prejudice indicated by these statistics. "Tell me why am I being treated like this for a crime I never committed?" asked high school student Amal Alomari. "Why is it that every time I go outside, people scream and yell at me. Why, because of the scarf that's on my head? I never did anything to cause people to look at me in such an ugly way. I'm an American teenager just like anyone else."

Amal argues that like major religions, Islam does not preach violence and hatred; rather, it treasures the "inherent dignity bestowed by God upon all human beings . . ." This view is expressed in a particular verse of the Qur'an: "Whoever kills a human being for other than manslaughter or corruption and mischief in the earth, it shall be as if he had killed all mankind, and whoever saves the life of one, it shall be as if he had saved the life or all mankind."

Hannah Hawk, a spokeswoman for the Muslim Public Affairs Council of Houston, Texas, sees few differences between the values of Islam and those of other religions practiced in the United States. "We believe in heaven and hell, in doing good deeds, in following the Ten Commandments," she says. "Islamic values are not only compatible with American values, they're almost identical."

War on Terrorism

The U.S. government acted swiftly and decisively following the terrorist attacks in 2001 and declared a war on terrorism. Armed forces were quickly dispatched to Afghanistan, where they rooted out fighters in the al-Qaeda terrorist network, led by a

A Haven from Religious Intolerance

The first settlers who arrived to America were seeking a haven from religious intolerance. These who settled Massachusetts, Pennsylvania, and other colonies championed religious views that were not accepted by the state religions in Europe. They decided to make the harrowing voyage across the Atlantic Ocean, heading for a new home where they could practice their faiths without fear of persecution.

The United States, however, did not become the ideal haven that the founding fathers envisioned. Prejudices have remained a part of many people's lives throughout U.S. history. During the historic presidential campaign of 1960, for example, the mistrust that many Protestant people harbored against Catholics emerged during John F. Kennedy's campaign for president. People feared that if Kennedy, a Catholic, won the election, Pope John XXIII would gain influence force over U.S. policy. After Kennedy became president those anxieties, of course, were revealed to be unfounded.

To an even greater extent, Jews have also experienced prejudice in the United States. Anti-Semitic hate crimes still occur today. In 1995, the Anti-Defamation League, an organization dedicated to tracking prejudice against religious minorities, conducted an audit of hate incidents against Jews on college campuses. The study spanned 10 years, beginning in 1984, and concluded that the number of attacks had risen over that period. There were 139 more anti-Semitic attacks in 1994 than there were in 1984.

There were some improvements, however, regarding attitudes toward Jewish students and their culture. "In recent decades, Jews have generally found the American campus to be a positive environment," said an ADL report. "Gone are the days of quotas limiting the number of Jewish students at our nation's top colleges and universities. It is now common to find flourishing Jewish life on many campuses." However, the same ADL report pointed out that schools are still susceptible to prejudice and extremist thinking. "In recent years, campuses have become a new proving ground for the tactics of all manner of extremists, forcing some colleges and universities onto the frontline in the fight against extremism and anti-Semitism."

Practitioners of non-traditional religions are also susceptible to hate crimes. A series of such incidents took place in Tennessee in 2002, compelling the parents of 14-year-old India Tracy to file a federal lawsuit the following year against the Union County School District. The Tracys, who practice paganism, claimed their daughter was harassed because of her religious beliefs. Paganism is an ancient religious tradition that embraces kinship with nature, respect for all people and religions, and the idea that God has both feminine and masculine natures. The American Religion Identification Survey estimates that more than 300,000 people practice paganism in the United States.

Many people equate paganism with witchcraft and Satanism. According to the Tracys' lawsuit, for three years India was harassed by other students, who called her a "Satan worshipper" and accused her of eating babies. She found slurs painted on her locker and was occasionally physically assaulted and injured by classmates. Throughout this time, the suit said, the school district took no disciplinary action against the harassers. According to India, in January 2002 three boys chased her down a hall in her middle school, grabbed her neck and said, "You better change your religion or we'll change it for you." Said her father, Greg Tracy, "That was pretty much the last straw because she was terrified." The Tracys took India out of the school, and while looking for another public school to attend, she stayed at home and took classes on the Internet.

Occasionally, hate crimes are so serious that the Civil Rights Division of the U.S. Justice Department must intervene. The division will file lawsuits in cases where it believes discrimination has violated an individual's right to worship. In some reported cases, acts of discrimination have led to reconciliation within a community. In 1997, three teenagers were arrested in Newtown, Pennsylvania, for smashing the front window and electric menorah displayed in a Jewish family's home. While police investigated, most of the family's Christian neighbors displayed menorahs in front of their homes in a show of solidarity. One of the teens arrested for the vandalism, Daniel Hudson, was ordered by a judge to write an essay about anti-Semitism, watch *Schindler's List*—an Academy Award–winning film about the Holocaust—and perform 250 hours of community service. To fulfill his service requirement, Hudson was assigned to clean the grounds and mow the lawn of a nearby synagogue. "I hurt people," Hudson said at his sentencing. "Now I want to do something to make up for it."

Nevertheless, prejudice continues to be part of the fabric of American society. Following the terrorist acts of 2001, as news organizations started reporting acts of prejudice against Muslim Americans, the country's Catholics, Jews, and other groups who have been the victims of hate could only wonder how such reports could come as a shock to anyone.

Saudi Arabian billionaire named Osama bin Laden. American troops also unseated the fundamentalist Taliban government that had been shielding some of bin Laden's al-Qaeda terrorists.

In 2003, the war on terrorism was extended to Iraq. The administration of President George W. Bush charged Iraq with sponsoring international terrorism and stockpiling nuclear, chemical, and biological weapons. In early April, Hussein's regime was quickly toppled by an international coalition led by American and British forces. It was a move supported by 60 percent of teens, according to a Gallup Youth Survey taken before the war. But despite the explanations of Islamic scholars about the international Muslim community, to many American teens watching the news coverage, all Muslims are Arab and bitterly opposed to the United States.

Not all Muslim Americans are immigrants from Middle Eastern countries. No question, many Muslims have immigrated to the United States to escape the repressive regimes of Middle Eastern countries. However, the American Religion Identification Survey found that of the some 3.5 million Americans who claim Arab heritage, just a quarter of them are Muslims. The remaining 75 percent are mostly Christians, including a large population of Christian Lebanese, Iraqis,

Egyptians, and Syrians who immigrated to the United States to escape religious persecution in their countries. "Put simply," ARIS said, "the majority of Arab Americans are not Muslims and the majority of Muslims are not Arab Americans."

The State Department estimates that 26 percent of the 6 million Muslim Americans immigrated from Middle East countries, while another 25 percent immigrated from South Asian countries such as India, Pakistan, Bangladesh, Sri Lanka, and Afghanistan. Other

After the September 2001 terrorist attacks, some Muslim American teens received taunts in public, in the midst of everyday activities.

NO ATHEISTS IN THE BOY SCOUTS

Occasionally, victims of religious persecution are those with no religion at all. Darrell Lambert of Tacoma, Washington, was a dedicated Boy Scout and an atheist. During the 10 years he was involved in Scouting, the 19-year-old earned 37 merit badges and the coveted rank of Eagle Scout, the organization's highest honor. In 2001 he was an assistant troop leader until the Scouts took away his membership, on the grounds that he did not believe in God.

The Boy Scouts of America is a private organization and as such has the right to decide who qualifies for membership. Scouts are taught the Boy Scout Law, which outlines the traits every Scout is expected to embody. According to the *Boy Scout Handbook*, "A Scout is reverent toward God. He is faithful in his religious duties. He respects the beliefs of others."

Darrell's atheism became public knowledge in October 2001. He had voiced his disapproval when a Scout leader made a comment about the need to ban atheists from Scouting. "Legally, [the Scouts] have a right to discriminate," Darrell told a reporter. "Morally they don't. That's what I'm fighting. They can't teach good citizenship and practice bad citizenship." Mark Hunter, a Boy Scout spokesman, defended the organization's decision, stating that "duty to God is one of our founding principles. It's been that way for 92 years."

Darrell appealed the Boy Scout's decision and lost. In his letter of appeal he said his dismissal was "un-Scout-like and un-American" and argued that "morals come from more than a belief in God." Gregg Shields, national spokesman for the Boy Scouts of America, said that Scouting is based on traditional American family values and that neither atheists nor homosexuals, who are also banned by the Scouts, are "the kinds of role models we'd choose to present to our youth."

Muslims have immigrated from East Asian countries such as Indonesia, the Philippines, Malaysia, and Thailand. In addition, the State Department said, about 35 percent of Muslim Americans are native-born, and a majority of them are African American. Yet even with Arab Americans making up such a small segment of the Muslim American population, their loyalties were still questioned following the September 2001 attacks.

Many young Muslim Americans found themselves confused by the backlash. "When I go to the mall or supermarkets, they don't look very welcoming," said Cymrrah Mohammad, a student at Belmont High School in Massachusetts. "Immediately after September 11, I noticed people uncomfortable with me, even children."

On the afternoon of the terrorist attacks on September 11, classes were dismissed early for Fareesa Abbasi and her schoolmates. Fareesa attended a private high school in Orland Park, Illinois. As an Indian—whom a misinformed individual may mistake for an Arab Muslim—Fareesa worried about her safety and the safety of some of her Indian friends. She offered to drive them home rather than let them walk. "My friend sitting next to me in the passenger seat wears a head scarf and, because of that, nasty things occurred," Fareesa said to a reporter. "Drivers in huge sport utility vehicles were trying to hit my car and run me off the road; some started swearing and honking at us. . . . Panicked, I turned on the radio for comfort. The DJ announced that Arabs were the prime suspects of committing the terrorist acts."

At Fatima Haque's high school prom, some of the girls told a news reporter that they experienced similar acts of prejudice—even in the hallways of the high school. With young Muslims already facing the challenges of adapting to a new culture and preserving their Islamic faith, suffering this intolerance only makes such obstacles seem even greater.

Chapter Eight

A 13-year-old Jewish girl celebrates her new commitment to the faith at a bat mitzvah (Jewish boys celebrate the bar mitzvah). Teen children of interfaith marriages may have to face complex questions about their own religious views.

Finding Their Own Faith

Wilson Baer worried that his father may not come to his upcoming bar mitzvah, the religious ceremony that celebrates a Jewish boy's 13th birthday and his new commitment to the faith. Wilson's parents are divorced and live in two cities—one in Lenox, Massachusetts, the other in Nantucket—and he doesn't see his father as much as he would like. But there is more than geography that separates the two. Wilson's father was raised as a Presbyterian, and Wilson's mother comes from a Jewish family. While the parents were married, the Baers celebrated both Jewish and Christian holidays. Wilson went to Hebrew school every week, but he also celebrated Christmas and Easter with his father's family.

The parents' divorce significantly changed things. Wilson's mother and father no longer celebrated each other's holidays, leaving Wilson to sort things out for himself. Explaining his situation in an essay for Interfaithfamily.com, a support group website, he wrote:

> I really want my dad to come to my bar mitzvah because becoming a bar mitzvah means that I have completed an important part of Jewish learning, and to me it would feel like something was missing if my dad weren't there. Even though my dad doesn't associate with Judaism anymore, I hope he realizes that my bar mitzvah is not only about Judaism, but is a real part of me. My dad will probably be there because he is proud of me. And if he doesn't come, I will be very disappointed, but I know he will still be there within my soul.

Wilson's dilemma is a relatively new one in the 5,000-year history of the Jewish people. For thousands of years, Jewish people typically married within the faith because they sought a common cultural identity. There were also external restrictions that stipulated whom they could marry, as well as where they could live and what kind of businesses they could practice.

In the United States, however, where Jews make up less than 2 percent of the overall population, assimilation has been more common. In 1960, 6 percent of Jews wed non-Jews; in 2001, about 50 percent of Jews wed outside their faith. Earlier in the 20th century, it was typical for Jewish parents to be distraught when one of their children announced he or she planned to marry outside the faith. To express their total disapproval, Jewish parents would do what as known as "sitting shiva" for the child, mourning as if the child had died. Today the American Jewish Committee, a Jewish interest organization, says only 12 percent of Jews oppose intermarriage, and more than half of all Jewish Americans say they would be accepting of their children's non-Jewish spouses.

In the past, other religious groups have looked askance at members who marry outside the faith. Theologian Martin Marty can remember a time in the 1940s when a Catholic-Lutheran union warranted exile from his Midwestern hometown. Now it merits only a shrug. "Even if a staunch Catholic marries a Methodist," he said, "there's almost a sigh of relief by the families that at least their child isn't marrying a druggy or a cult member."

According to *USA Today*, nearly a quarter of U.S. households are made up of couples in mixed marriages. Today's young people appear willing to accept intermarriage. A Gallup Youth Survey released in 2002 reported that 79 percent of respondents said they

Marriages between people of different faiths—particularly between sects of a religion—are more common today than in past eras.

"feel comfortable being with people whose ideas, beliefs and values are different from their own." Joel Crohn, an expert on intermarriage, estimated that 21 percent of Catholics were in mixed marriages in 1990, as were 30 percent of Mormons and 40 percent of Muslims.

Some interfaith families raise their children in a faith of one of the parents; others totally ignore the issue of faith, while still others expose the children to both faiths. Stephen and Eileen Smith, who live in Chicago, raise their children as Catholics and Jews. Their three children, all under age 11, attend two services every weekend—one at a synagogue and the other at a church. Eileen, the Catholic, told *Newsweek*, "We don't do soccer. We do church." Stephen expects the children will eventually choose one of the two religions when they are older.

Leslie Goodman-Malamuth, author of a book for interfaith children, thinks this strategy is unwise. She says, "Children of intermarriage often feel they're not as good as their all-Jewish or all-Christian cousins. They feel like damaged goods." The child who rejects dad's religion may feel as though he or she were rejecting dad as well.

Seventeen-year-old Elissa Oblath-Johnsrud would probably disagree. The Los Angeles teen has a father who was reared in a fundamentalist Christian sect and a mother who is Jewish. The couple agreed to raise Elissa as a Jew, and even after they divorced, they continued on the path of mediating between the two religions. Today, Elissa considers herself a Jew but does not care if she marries someone out of the faith.

The rise in intermarriage and the subsequent blurring of the lines between different faiths has significant implications, as changes in the country's religious fabric are sure to affect the country's political and social landscape. One of the first studies of people in interfaith marriages, performed in 2001 by the American Religion Identification Survey, observed the spiritual lives of 50,000 adults over the age of 18. Researchers discovered that couples with children in interfaith marriages are three times more likely to divorce than couples who share the same faith.

Divorce mediator Rabbi Jeffrey Marx says religion is nearly always a factor in the divorce cases of interfaith couples. Sometimes it takes a court of law to settle the spouses' religious disputes. That's what happened with Jeffrey and Barbara Kendall, an interfaith couple living in Massachusetts who wanted a divorce. Jeffrey, a non-practicing Catholic, had married Barbara, a Reformed Jew, and agreed that their children would be brought up in the Jewish faith. Neither of them thought the religious divide would be a crucial factor in the marriage, but neither could have predicted that each would have a religious awakening.

They found themselves deeply divided when Jeffrey began attending a fundamentalist Christian church and Barbara started going to a more conservative synagogue. Fundamentalist Christians believe in the literal meaning of the Bible and, thus, often conflict with those who reject the claim that Jesus Christ is the savior of humanity. Around the time that Jeffrey's faith grew, Barbara gave up Reform Judaism for the much more conservative sect of Judaism known as Orthodox. The Orthodox branch of Judaism is among the religion's strictest, and in most cases, Orthodox Jews frown on marrying out of the faith.

The Kendalls reached the point where there was no longer any room for give-and-take between them, owing to the great disparity between their newfound beliefs. Jeffrey believed his wife would not go to heaven because she did not accept Jesus, yet their three children, Moriah, Ariel, and Rebekah, all under age eight, were being raised as Orthodox Jews. They ate kosher food and observed the Sabbath on Saturdays, and the two boys had grown their hair in long forelocks called *payes*. Meanwhile, Jeffrey had told his children that their mother was damned for denying the Gospel's message.

The couple's divorce dispute dragged on for three years until 1997, when the Massachusetts Supreme Court granted them a divorce with an unusual warning: Jeffrey could no longer share his religious beliefs with his children because they were making the children uncomfortable. Martha Minow, a Harvard Law professor, said that the controversial verdict was not an easy one. "It pits one fundamental right—the right to parent—against another fundamental right—the right of religious free exercise," she said.

Declining Rates of Affliliation

When parents of different faiths decide to raise their children in a single religion or denomination, some tend to take precedence over others. According to the ARIS, Catholicism seems to have the greatest advantage over other faiths. Sixty-six percent of inter-married Catholics said they are raising their children in the Catholic faith. The numbers for Protestants in a similar situation are also high, with 54 percent of intermarried Lutherans and 51 percent of intermarried Methodists raising children in their respective faiths.

Twenty-two percent of the U.S. adult population lives in a mixed religion household, the ARIS found. The rates were lowest for Mormons (12 percent), and members of the Baptist, Evangelical, Church of Christ, and Assembly of God denominations (18 percent). Buddhists represented 39 percent of mixed households and Episcopalians accounted for 42 percent.

Of all the major religions in the United States, Judaism has experienced the biggest decline in practitioners as a result of intermarriage. Jews are losing so many members—to other religions or no religion at all—that some experts predict the American Jewish community may shrink to one-third or even

The numbers of Jewish people marrying out of the faith are growing, a trend that is threatening the practice of religious traditions among Jewish American children and teens.

one-sixth of its present size within two generations.

A 2001 study of 235,000 Jewish freshmen, conducted by Professor Linda Sax of UCLA's Higher Education Research Institute, further illustrates this drop-off rate. The survey compared the Jewish students' answers to data collected from 5 million non-Jewish freshmen since 1971. In the largest study ever dedicated to Jewish freshmen, data indicated that 93 percent of students with two Jewish parents thought of themselves as Jewish. If their mother was Jewish but their father was not, 38 percent of the teens identified themselves as Jews;

if their father was Jewish but their mother was not, 15 percent of the freshmen thought of themselves as Jews.

Jeff Rubin, director of communications for Hillel, the Jewish outreach foundation active on 110 college campuses, observes a gap between the practices of today's Jewish students and those of past years. "The largest number of students we serve have not had a Jewish background in the way that was traditionally defined — through Jewish history, culture and commitment to Jewish observance," he said. In the coming years, devoted Jews hope that the younger generations will show a renewed interest in the history, culture, and traditions of the Jewish faith.

Glossary

ATHEISTS—People who are certain God does not exist.

BAR MITZVAH—The coming-of-age ceremony for 13-year-old Jewish males in which they lead services, read from the Torah, and assume the obligations of being an adult in their congregation. The corresponding ceremony for 12- and 13-year-old girls is known as a bat mitzvah.

DISEMBOWELED—The physical state in which someone's bowels have been removed.

KOSHER—A description of food that has been prepared in accordance with Jewish dietary laws.

MENORAH—The candleholder displayed by Jewish families during the holiday known as Hanukkah.

MONOTHEISTIC—Having the belief that there is only one God.

PLAINTIFF—In court, the person who brings a lawsuit alleging that a wrong has been done to him or her.

QUR'AN (OR KORAN)—The sacred text of Islam containing the word of God as told to the Prophet Muhammad.

SHIVA—A Jewish mourning ritual in which family and friends gather to honor the memory of the dead. Mourners sometimes cover their mirrors, rip their clothing, and avoid music and merriment.

SWASTIKA—A cross with four arms that served as the symbol of Nazi Germany.

TORAH—The sacred text of the Jewish religion encompassing the Five Books of Moses.

VALEDICTORIAN—A high school senior with the highest grade-point average who is also given the honor of addressing fellow students at graduation.

YOM KIPPUR—Jewish holiday in which participants fast for 24 hours while they attend services and ask for forgiveness for the sins they have committed.

Further Reading

Alley, Robert S. *School Prayer: The Court, the Congress, and the First Amendment.* New York: Prometheus Books, 1994.

Armstrong, Karen. *The Battle for God: Fundamentalism in Judaism, Christianity and Islam.* New York: Random House, 2001.

Aydt, Rachel. *Why Me?: A Teen Guide to Divorce and Your Feelings.* New York: Rosen Publishing Group, 2000.

Bernall, Misty. *She Said Yes: The Unlikely Martyrdom of Cassie Bernall.* New York: Pocket Books, 2000.

Beshir, Ekram, and Mohamed Rida Beshir. *Muslim Teens: Today's Worry, Tomorrow's Hope.* Beltsville, Md: Amana Publications, 2001.

Delgatto, Laurie. *She Said . . . He Said . . . : Teens Speak Out on Life and Faith.* Winona, Minn.: St. Mary's Press, 2003.

Gastfriend, Edward. *My Father's Testament: Memoir of a Jewish Teenager: 1938–1945.* Philadelphia: Temple University Press, 2000.

George, Elizabeth. *A Young Woman After God's Heart: A Teen's Guide to Friends, Faith, Family, and the Future.* Eugene, Oreg.: Harvest House, 2003.

Kamlin, Ben. *Raising a Thoughtful Teenager.* New York: Dutton, 1996.

Nimmo, Beth, and Darrell Scott. *Rachel's Tears: The Spiritual Journey of Columbine Martyr Rachel Scott.* Nashville, Tenn.: Thomas Nelson Publishers, 2000.

Noll, James William. *Taking Sides: Clashing Views on Controversial Educational Issues.* Guilford, Conn.: McGraw-Hill/Dushkin, 2003.

Novak, Phillip. *The World's Wisdom: Sacred Texts of the World's Religions.* New York: HarperCollins, 1995.

Petsonk, Judy, and Jim Remsen. *The Intermarriage Handbook: A Guide for Jews and Christians.* New York: Arbor House-William Morrow, 1988.

Further Reading

Smith, Huston. *The World's Religions: Our Great Wisdom Traditions.* New York: HarperCollins, 1991.

Talk, DC, and Voice of the Martyrs. *Jesus Freaks: Stories of Those Who Stood for Jesus.* Grand Rapids, Mich.: Bethany House, 1999.

Youngs, Bettie B, Jennifer Leigh Youngs, and Debbie Thurman. *A Teen's Guide to Christian Living: Practical Answers to Tough Questions About God and Faith.* Deerfield Beach, Fla.: Faith Communications, 2003

Zoba, Wendy Murray. *Generation 2K: What Parents and Others Need to Know About the Millennials.* Downers Grove, Ill.: InterVarsity Press, 1999.

Internet Resources

http://www.gallup.com

The Gallup Organization's web site features information on the Gallup Youth Surveys as well as the other polling work conducted by the organization. Access latest poll results on stories relating to religion and values and read teens' views on the subject.

http://www.religioustolerance.org/equ_acce.htm

Prepared by the Religious Tolerance Organization, this page gives an excellent overview of the Equal Access Act, its wording, and what schools should and should not be doing. The site also offers many interesting links.

http://www.adl.org/religion_ps/default.asp

On this page the Anti-Defamation League, an organization that defends the rights of religious minorities, discusses religion in schools. Among the topics discussed are creationism, religion in classrooms, and the constitutionality of displaying the Ten Commandments in schools and other public buildings.

http://www.belief.net

The Internet site, run by a "multi-faith e-community," includes a special section for teens, daily quotes from the Dalai Lama, a spirituality survey, and online prayer circles to join.

http://www.Islam101.com

An online course in Islam covering the religion, its culture, and views on contemporary issues. Read about the Qur'an, Islam and science, art, terrorism, and prominent Muslims.

http://www.himalayanacademy.com

This home page of Hinduism Online answers the nine most common questions asked about Hinduism. It also explains the basics of the religion and how one can become a practicing Hindu.

Internet Resources

http://www.gc.suny.edu./studies

The home page of the American Religion Identification Study. Read a summary of the findings of the study conducted by the City University of New York or check out the entire report.

http://www.awesomestories.com/religion/index2.htm

A collection of links to pages covering the historical figures and stories of the major religions. It also features links to discussions of central issues like freedom of religion.

Publisher's Note: The websites listed in this book were active at the time of publication. The publisher is not responsible for websites that have changed their address or discontinued operation since the date of publication. The publisher reviews and updates the websites each time the book is reprinted.

Index

Numbers in **bold italic** refer to captions and graphs.

Index

Index

Index

Picture Credits

Contributors

GEORGE GALLUP JR. is chairman of The George H. Gallup International Institute (sponsored by The Gallup International Research and Education Center, or GIREC) and is senior scientist and member of the GIREC council. Mr. Gallup serves as chairman of the board of the National Coalition for Children's Justice and as a trustee of the National Fatherhood Initiative. He serves on many other boards in the area of health, education and religion.

Mr. Gallup is recognized internationally for his research and study on youth, health, religion, and urban problems. He has written numerous books including *My Kids On Drugs?* with Art Linkletter (Standard, 1981), *The Great American Success Story* with Alec Gallup and William Proctor (Dow Jones-Irwin, 1986), *Growing Up Scared in America* with Wendy Plump (Morehouse, 1995), *Surveying the Religious Landscape: Trends in U.S. Beliefs* with D. Michael Lindsay (Morehouse, 1999), and *The Next American Spirituality* with Timothy Jones (Chariot Victor Publishing, 1999).

Mr. Gallup received his BA degree from the Princeton University Department of Religion in 1954, and holds seven honorary degrees. He has received many awards, including the Charles E. Wilson Award in 1994, the Judge Issacs Lifetime Achievement Award in 1996, and the Bethune-DuBois Institute Award in 2000. Mr. Gallup lives near Princeton, New Jersey, with his wife, Kingsley. They have three grown children.

THE GALLUP YOUTH SURVEY was founded in 1977 by Dr. George Gallup to provide ongoing information on the opinions, beliefs and activities of America's high school students and to help society meet its responsibility to youth. The topics examined by the Gallup Youth Survey have covered a wide range—from abortion to zoology. From its founding through the year 2001, the Gallup Youth Survey sent more than 1,200 weekly reports to the Associated Press, to be distributed to newspapers around the nation. Since January 2002, Gallup Youth Survey reports have been made available on a weekly basis through the Gallup Tuesday Briefing.

GAIL SNYDER has written several books for young readers. Her other title in the Gallup Youth Survey series is *Teens and Alcohol*. She has also written about George Washington's childhood and the nation of Sudan. Gail lives with her husband, Hal Marcovitz, their children Ashley and Michelle, and her father, Aaron Snyder, in Chalfont, Pennsylvania.